BITCOIN IS JUST THE BEGINNING!

It's Not Too Late to Start Investing and Trading in Crypto Currencies

Keith Croteau

FREE MEMBERSHIP BONUS

Since Bitcoin was only the beginning and cryptocurrencies (CC) are still in their infancy phase, we've created a website that will offer valuable information for your education on what we consider the biggest innovation since the Internet.

In addition, since the blockchain software used by cryptocurrencies will most likely dominate the world economy and probably become the "FUTURE OF FINANCE," we are developing our website to be the most informative in this sector.

Since you took the time to "READ THE FIRST PAGE" (aha) of our book, you will receive a free membership.

Your Free 60-Day Membership will include:

- Access to the Elite Platinum Level Content
- 2 Personal Consultation Calls (1/month)
- Unlimited Updates by Text Message for Altcoin Buy & Sell Alerts
- All New Reference Material That We Release (Shipping Charges Not Included)

Don't delay! Get your
FREE MEMBERSHIP TODAY

VISIT:

www.cryptosecretinfo.com/bookbonus

COPYRIGHT

RCI Acquisitions, Inc.
24310 Moulton Parkway, Suite O-196
Laguna Hills, CA 92637

Limits of Liability and Disclaimer of Warranty

The author and publisher shall not be liable for your misuse of this material. This book is for strictly informational and educational purposes.

Disclaimer

The views expressed are those of the author/Webmaster and do not reflect the official policy or position of the Cryptocurrency Exchanges or Cryptocurrency Companies or Management.

Copyright Use and Public Information

Unless otherwise noted, images have been used with permission and are in keeping with public information laws. Please contact the author for questions about copyrights or the use of public information.

Interior Design: Eric D. Groleau (Strategic Edge Innovations Publishing)
Edited By: Strategic Edge Innovations Publishing (SEI.im)

ISBN: 978-0986311260

ABOUT THE AUTHOR

KEITH CROTEAU was born and raised in South Florida and received a Bachelor of Science Degree in Education from Florida Atlantic University. He has since built and sold many successful companies.

With the wisdom to move from one industry to the next, he has transitioned his small lawn service to a 20-acre foliage nursery shipping plants nationwide. After selling the land and company, he went into the payphone business and had over 25,000 phones across the country managed by more than 80 employees.

Realizing the future was heading to the Internet, he moved into telecommunications services for small to medium-size business and hotels. Simultaneously, Keith opened four retail cellular stores and invested in Real Estate. Leveraging his business expertise, he has been a Business Consultant, Coach, and Mentor for many small business owners.

Keith began researching Bitcoin & Cryptocurrencies in 2014. He has since invested, made huge profits and started to guide his closest friends in this realm. His inner circle of friends has greatly profited from his knowledge and his Crypto-Insider Picks.

"THE TIME HAS NOW COME TO TEACH & PASS ON HIS CRYPTO KNOWLEDGE TO A WIDER AUDIENCE USING THIS BOOK."

CONTENTS

DEDICATION

This book is dedicated to the 3rd millennium
"New Age Investors…"

… Individuals who are set to believe in the process
and will stop at nothing to get there!

PART 1:

THE HISTORY OF BITCOIN

CRYPTOCURRENCIES

& ALTCOINS

The NY Times has Provided the Majority of the historical information for this chapter

Bitcoin — The Beginning

October 2008:

An idea is born. A person, or perhaps a group of people, going by the name Satoshi Nakamoto publishes a paper outlining a peer-to-peer electronic cash system.

The idea represents a breakthrough in using software code to authenticate and protect transactions without resorting to a centralized bank or government treasury.

January 2009:

The Bitcoin (BC) network came into existence with the release of the first open source (BC) client and the issuance of the first (BC), with Satoshi Nakamoto mining the first block of (BC) ever (known as the genesis block), which had a reward of 50 (BC).

Kristoffer Koch bought 5,000 (BC) in 2009 for **$27**, now worth **$886,000**. Talk about a degree that gives you bang for your buck. Koch was writing a thesis on encryption in 2009 when he spent about **$27** to buy 5,000 (BC).

May 2010:

A person uses (BC) to order pizza three months after a marketplace was established for the currency. The pizza cost him/her 10,000 (BC).

An image posted to a (BC) forum by a user named Laszlo claiming to have bought the first pizza using the alternative currency.

July 2012:

Despite risks, the use of the currency grows, but it's largely relegated to corners of the Internet, including black markets that sell illegal goods.

Nonetheless, several enterprising groups begin devising ways to legitimize (BC), including the Paly Entrepreneurs Club, an extracurricular group at a high school in Palo Alto, Calif., that works to organize a trading network for the currency. Coinbase, a Silicon Valley start-up, also aims to provide a non-technical solution to using (BC).

Peter DeSilva—NY Times

April 2013:

After a price surge that began in January, the collective value of (BC) goes over a billion dollars. That is a lot of coins in any form, and the billion-dollar milestone turns the once-obscure online currency into a media sensation.

So why the sudden surge in value? Some point to the recent economic crisis in the European Union, which makes a currency beyond the control of governments more tempting. And as with a run-up in anything tradable—tulip bulbs, dot-com shares—there is also the hypnotic logic that says the price went up today, so that means it will go up tomorrow.

What is clear, however, is that the main use of the currency appears to be illicit activity. There are online gambling sites that use (BC) and anonymous online marketplace Silk Road, which accepts only (BC), is "overwhelmingly used as a market for controlled substances and narcotics," according to a paper on Silk Road written by a Carnegie Mellon professor.

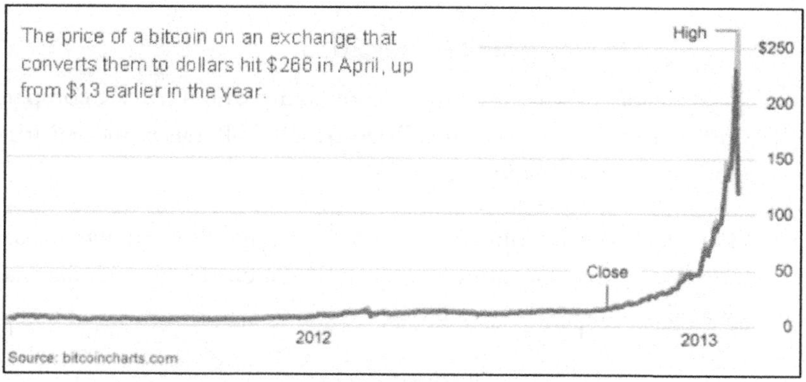

The Winklevoss twins, Cameron and Tyler—Olympic rowers, nemeses of Mark Zuckerberg—amass what appears to be one of the single largest portfolios of the digital currency. The Winklevii, as they are known, said that they own nearly $11 million worth of [BC]. In addition to the twins, Silicon Valley investment firms, while not holding (BC), are starting to show interest in the technology.

July 2013:

The Winklevosses file a proposal with securities regulators that would allow any investor to trade (BC) just as if they were stocks. It involves an exchange-traded fund, which usually tracks a basket of stocks or a commodity, but in this case will hold only (BC).

It is part of a broader effort to remove the stigma hovering over (BC) and other online money endeavors. They are facing a barrage of regulatory questions and enforcement actions.

Just about this time, the world's largest trading exchange for (BC), Mt. Gox, files with the Treasury Department to register itself as a money services business and comply with money-laundering laws.

A Texas man, Trendon T. Shavers, is sued by the SEC and accused of running a Ponzi scheme that collected (BC) from investors, promising them seven percent weekly returns.

Mr. Shaver was selling some of the (BC) and using the proceeds for his "rent, car-related expenses, utilities, retail purchases, casinos, and meals," according to the complaint.

September 2013:

SecondMarket, which allows investors to buy shares of hot private companies like Twitter, started Betting on the Price of (BC). It raises money for an investment fund that will hold only (BC).

The fund, the Bitcoin Investment Trust, aims to provide a reliable and easy way to bet on the future price of (BC), a currency generally traded on unregulated, online exchanges based overseas.

October 2013:

Silk Road, a black market powered by Bitcoins, is shut down. FBI agents arrest Ross Ulbricht, 29, the man believed to be behind the Silk Road marketplace, on narcotics and money-laundering charges.

Silk Road began in 2011 as an underground online marketplace for drug users, a site where endless varieties of marijuana—as well as LSD, ecstasy and prescription pills—could be bought from sellers across the world.

It worked on one principle: Everyone remained anonymous. Users could gain access to the network only through software meant to ensure anonymity. Credit cards and PayPal were not accepted. Bitcoins, a virtual currency, were, and even those transactions were scrambled.

Silk Road is believed to have been responsible for something approaching half of all transactions involving Bitcoins.

Moving Mainstream, a Bitcoin A.T.M., Opens in Vancouver. The kiosk, which looks like an average ATM but with hand and barcode scanners, opens for business at a trendy coffee shop in Vancouver, British Columbia.

With the ATM, users scan their hand to confirm their identity, then funds move to or from a virtual wallet on their smartphone. The system limits transfers to $1,000 a day, in an effort to curb money laundering and other fraud.

November 2013:

Value Surpasses $700. The price of a (BC) on an exchange that converts them to dollars rises to $780, a meteoric gain from its beginnings in 2010. The total outstanding pool of Bitcoin—which is created by a network of users who solve complex mathematical problems—is now worth more than $7 billion.

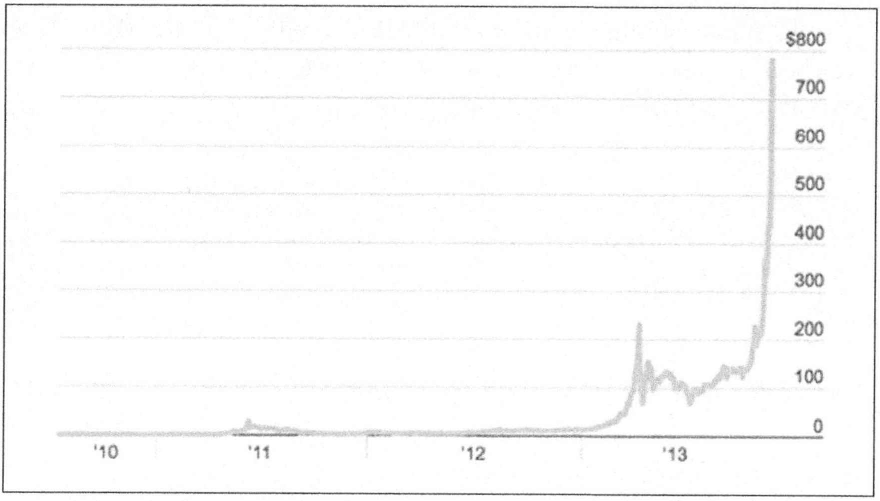

February 2014:

Bitcoin is currently trading at near $250 and it got as low as $220.29 from a high of $540. Once the largest platform for trading Bitcoin, Mt. Gox recently halted withdrawals, which exacerbated fears about having wealth in the digital currency.

The good news for Bitcoin adherents is that the currency is still trading near $600 on other exchanges. Mt. Gox, once the gold standard of Bitcoin exchanges, has been having technical problems.

Coinbase, a (BC) Exchange, is now becoming the gold standard. "Prices remain volatile and market illiquidity high. If Bitcoin currency and infrastructure are unstable, it is increasingly dangerous to subject the global economy to such market risk uncertainty. The longer the virtual currency economy is allowed to grow unchecked, the greater the potential of adverse economic impact."

Bitcoin 2015:

After a year filled with its share of doom and gloom, the verdict is in: Bitcoin won 2015. As trumpeted by headlines in *CNBC*, and *Bloomberg*, Bitcoin is the best-performing currency of the year, netting near-40% gains, more than twice its nearest competition, the Somali shilling and Gambian dalasi. The development contrasts with Bitcoin's performance from 2014, in which it lost 56% of its value, the highest drop among global currencies.

A look at the CoinDesk USD Bitcoin Price Index (BPI) from October on reveals an impressive upward arch that contrasts with the choppy peaks and valleys of earlier months.

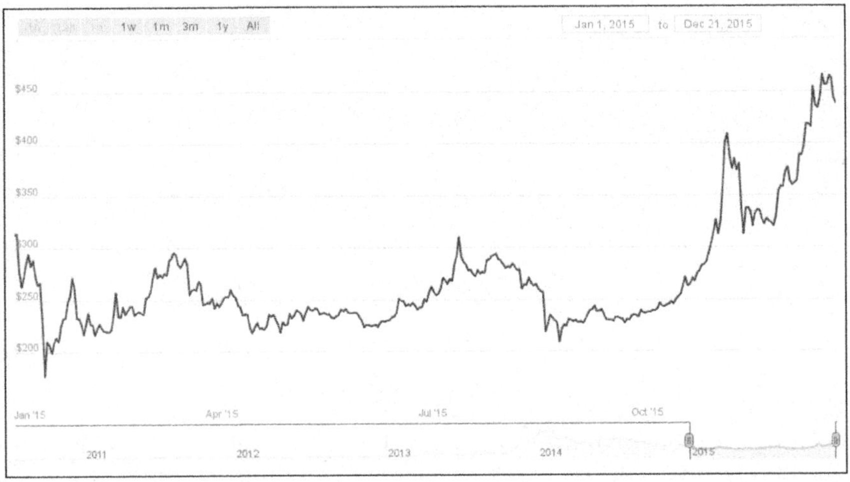

December 2015. So, here we are in the closing month of 2015, and the price is trending up. On the 15th, it reached the highest level since September December 2014, climbing to more than $465 across most major exchanges.

Bitcoin 2016-17:

The biggest gains in the history of the Bitcoin happened during this period. People who never thought they would be millionaires became millionaires. I started investing in March 2017 and have made more money in 2017 just from cryptocurrency [CC] than any year of my life and I'm 62 years old. The next chart shows all assets such as stocks, Bonds, Gold, Silver, etc. trends that have been happening over the course of time. Bitcoin and Altcoins will be no different.

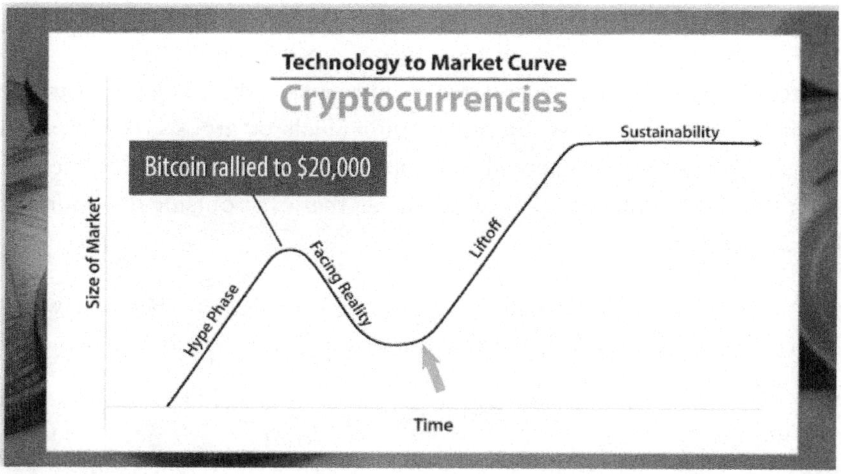

The (BC) price index is an average of (BC) prices across leading global exchanges.

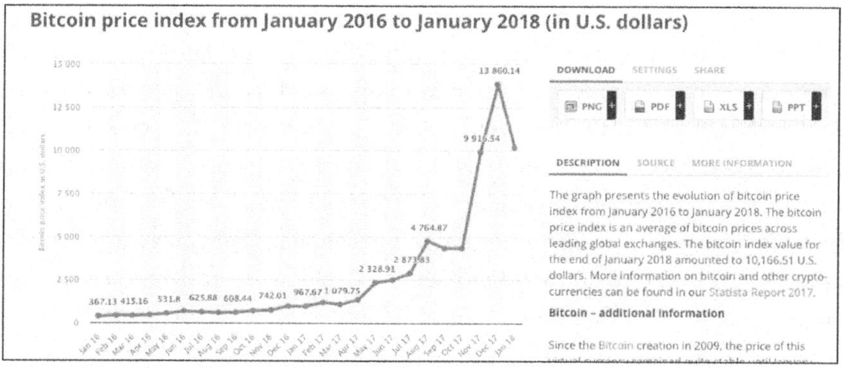

Cryptocurrency — The Reasons Behind It

Cryptocurrencies (CC), or virtual currencies, are digital means of exchange created and used by private individuals or groups. Because most (CC) aren't regulated by national governments, they're considered alternative currencies—mediums of financial exchange that exist outside the bounds of state monetary policy.

Bitcoin is the preeminent (CC), and the first to be used widely. However, hundreds of (CC) exist, and more spring into being every month.

What Is (CC)?

Cryptocurrencies use cryptographic protocols, or extremely complex code systems that encrypt sensitive data transfers, to secure their units of exchange. Cryptocurrency developers build these protocols on advanced mathematics and computer engineering principles that render them virtually impossible to break, or to duplicate or counterfeit the protected currencies. These protocols also mask the identities of (CC) users, making transactions and fund flows difficult to attribute to specific individuals or groups.

Cryptocurrencies are also marked by decentralized control. Cryptocurrencies' supply and value are controlled by the activities of their users and highly complex protocols built into their governing codes, not the conscious decisions of central banks or other regulatory authorities. In particular, the activities of miners — (CC) users who use vast amounts of computing power to record transactions, receiving newly created (CC) units and transaction fees paid by other users in return—are critical to currencies' stability and smooth function.

Importantly, (CC) can be exchanged for fiat currencies in special online markets, meaning each has a variable exchange rate with major world currencies (such as the U.S. dollar, British pound, European euro, and Japanese yen). Cryptocurrency exchanges are somewhat vulnerable to hacking and they are the most common venue for digital currency theft.

Most, but not all, (CC) are characterized by finite supply. Their source codes contain instructions outlining the precise number of units that can and will ever exist. Over time, it becomes more difficult for miners to produce (CC) units, until the upper limit is reached and new currency ceases to be minted altogether. Cryptocurrencies' finite supply makes them inherently deflationary, more akin to gold and other precious metals—of which there are finite supplies—than fiat currencies, which central banks can, in theory, produce unlimited supplies of.

Due to their political independence and essentially impenetrable data security, (CC) users enjoy benefits not available to users of traditional fiat currencies, such as the U.S. dollar, and the financial systems that those currencies support. For instance, whereas a government can easily freeze or even seize a bank account located in its jurisdiction, it's very difficult for it to do the same with funds held in (CC)—even if the holder is a citizen or legal resident.

On the other hand, (CC) come with a host of risks and drawbacks, such as illiquidity and value volatility, that don't affect many fiat currencies. Additionally, since (CC) are frequently used to facilitate gray and black-market transactions, many countries view them with distrust or outright animosity. While some proponents tout (CC) as potentially lucrative alternative investments, few (if any) serious financial professionals view them as suitable for anything other than pure speculation.

How Cryptocurrencies Work

The source codes and technical controls that support and secure (CC) are highly complex. However, laypeople are more than capable of understanding the basic concepts and becoming informed (CC) users.

Functionally, most (CC) are variations on (BC), the first widely used (CC). Like traditional currencies, (CC) express value in units—for instance, you can say "I have 2.5 Bitcoin," just as you'd say, "I have $2.50."

Blockchain [BLC]—How it All Started & What the Heck is it?

Many of the technologies we now take for granted were quiet revolutions in their time. Just think about how much smartphones have changed the way we live and work. It used to be that when people were out of the office, they were *gone,* because a telephone was tied to a place, not to a person. Now we have global nomads building new businesses straight from their phones. And to think: Smartphones have been around for merely a decade.

We're now in the midst of another quiet revolution: (BLC), a distributed database that maintains a continuously growing list of ordered records, called "blocks." Consider what's happened in just the past 10 years:

- The first major (BLC) innovation was (BC), a digital currency experiment. The market cap of (BC) now hovers between $10–20 billion, and it is used by millions of people for payments, including a large and growing remittances market.

- The second innovation was called (BLC), which was essentially the realization that the underlying technology that operated (BC) could be separated from the currency and used for all kinds of other inter-organizational cooperation. Almost every major financial institution in the world is doing (BLC) research at the moment, and 15% of banks are expected to be using (BLC) in 2017.

- The third innovation was called the "SMART CONTRACT" embodied in a second generation (BLC) system called Ethereum, which built little computer programs directly into (BLC) that allowed financial instruments, like loans or bonds, to be represented, rather than the cash-like tokens of the (BC). The Ethereum smart contract platform now has a market cap of around a billion dollars, with hundreds of projects headed toward the market.

- The fourth major innovation, the current cutting edge of (BLC) thinking, is called "proof of stake." Current generation (BLC) are secured by "proof of work," in which the group with the largest total computing power makes the decisions. These groups are called "miners" and operate vast data centers to provide this security, in exchange for (CC) payments. The new systems do away with these data centers, replacing them with complex financial instruments, for a similar or even higher degree of security. Proof-of-stake systems are expected to go live later this year.

- The fifth major innovation on the horizon is called (BLC) scaling. Right now, in the (BLC) world, every computer in the network processes every transaction. This is slow. A scaled (BLC) accelerates the process, without sacrificing security, by determining how many computers are necessary to validate each transaction and dividing up the work efficiently. To manage this without compromising the legendary security and robustness of (BLC) is a difficult problem, but not an intractable one. A scaled (BLC) is expected to be fast enough to power the Internet of things and go head-to-head with the major payment middlemen of the banking world (VISA and SWIFT).

This innovation landscape represents just 10 years of work by an elite group of computer scientists, cryptographers, and mathematicians. As the full potential of these breakthroughs hits society, things are sure to get a little weird. Self-driving cars and drones will use (BLC) to pay for services like charging stations and landing pads. International currency transfers will go from taking days to an hour, and then to a few minutes, with a higher degree of reliability than the current system has been able to manage.

These changes, among others, represent a pervasive lowering of transaction costs. When transaction costs drop past invisible thresholds, there will be sudden, dramatic, hard-to-predict aggregations and disaggregations of existing business models. For example, auctions used to be narrow and local, rather than universal and global, as they are now on sites like eBay. As the costs of reaching people dropped, there was a sudden change in the system. (BLC) is reasonably expected to trigger as many of these cascades as e-commerce has done since it was invented, in the late 1990s.

Predicting what direction this will all take is hard. Did anybody see social media coming? Who would have predicted that clicking on our friends' faces would replace time spent in front of the TV? Predictors usually overestimate how fast things will happen and underestimate the long-term impacts. But the sense of scale inside the (BLC) industry is that the changes coming will be "as large as the original invention of the Internet," and this may not be overstated. What we can predict is that as (BLC) matures and more people catch on to this new mode of collaboration, it will extend into everything from supply chains to provably fair Internet dating (eliminating the possibility of fake profiles and other underhanded techniques). And given how far (BLC) has come in 10 years, perhaps the future could indeed arrive sooner than any of us think.

Until the late 1990s, it was impossible to process a credit card securely on the Internet—e-commerce simply did not exist. How fast could (BLC) bring about another revolutionary change? Consider that Dubai's (BLC) strategy is to issue all government documents on (BLC) by 2020, with substantial initial projects just announced to go live this year. The Internet of Agreements concept, presented at the World Government Summit, builds on this strategy to envision a substantial transformation of global trade, using (BLC) to smooth out some of the bumps caused by Brexit and the recent U.S. withdrawal from the Trans-Pacific Partnership. These ambitious agendas will have to be proven in practice, but the expectation in Dubai is that cost savings and innovation benefits will more than justify the cost of experimentation. As Mariana Mazzucato teaches in *The Entrepreneurial State*, the cutting edge of innovation, particularly in infrastructure, is often in the hands of the state, and that idea seems destined to be true in the (BLC) space.

2018 The Year of the Altcoin

The Good, The Bad, and The Ugly

Altcoins are the alternative (CC) launched after the success of (BC). Generally, they project themselves as better substitutes to (BC). The success of (BC) as the first peer-to-peer digital currency paved the way for many to follow. There is a great variety of **altcoins**.

There's (BC), Ethereum, Ripple, Litecoin. (BC) Cash, Ripple, NEO, TRON, whatever! Any coin that is not (BC) would be an "ALTCOIN." Some investors believe that if it's not (BC), it's a scam! NOT TRUE!

There is some truth to that thought and of all the 1,000 (CC) out there, about 95% are complete money grabs or Ponzi Schemes and will disappear before you have a chance to get your money out. That's the "REAL TRUTH" as of this writing.

When you have a (BLC) code there is only one chain for a certain application. There are many that can be valuable to a certain market or niche. There will be no "ONE COIN TO RULE THEM ALL." There will be many winners and you just need to know how to find them.

With (CC) there are no geographical borders. Bitcoin & Ethereum, for instance, work just as well in every single part of the world.

In this section, we will see that beside (BC), the (CC) world is very wide and it is continuing to grow exponentially. If we look back at (BC) creation in 2009, we see that the first Altcoin came out only after two years. Then the rate of Altcoin launches started to grow only from 2013 and 2014. It went on increasing until now. In 2017, more than 600 new (CC) were created, so it has become impossible to check and study them all.

One important metric to understand Altcoin value is the Market Cap (CC) corresponding to the unitary cost multiplied by the number of coins in circulation. Using this metric (BC) is still the first, and Ethereum and Ripple occupy the next two places. It is possible to check the live situation on the

CoinMarketCap website.

However, every Altcoin has something that distinguishes it from others, such as differences in the scripting language, transactions management, additional features, or security, mining-based or not, with different consensus algorithms and other differences. They can also differ from (BC) simply because they have different built-in parameters, such as average time between the creation of blocks or blocks size.

Now let's dig deeper into some Altcoins stories.

Litecoin: first memory-hard mining puzzle:

Litecoin was born in 2011 sometime after Namecoin. For several years Litecoin was the second main (CC) after (BC). The main technical difference from (BC) is its mining puzzle. Litecoin uses a memory-hard mining puzzle, while the (BC) is a computation-hard one.

Dogecoin: having fun with (CC):

Dogecoin was born at the end of 2013. Besides a few technical changes from (BC), the main difference between Dogecoin and other currencies is that it was born with the purpose of having fun with (CC).

In fact, Dogecoin supported many marketing campaigns and public events, which let it to become popular in a short term after its launch.

For example, it appeared at:

- NASCAR
- 2014 Winter Olympic Games.

Now the Dogecoin block reward is fixed and halved every two months. Bottom line, there is "NO SINGLE SOLUTION" for one (CC) OR Altcoin.

Since the Altcoin space is what is facing the blunt end of the stick right now, this is where all of our collective eyes are. Yes, (BC) went through a potential fork on August 1, and that can impact both (BC) and the Altcoin's valuation for sure. We will likely see further turbulence when that does happen too … or perhaps the turbulence we're feeling is already baked in and partly due to August 1 anyway.

But the bigger picture is that (BC) is simply not the exclusive solution to disrupting currency anymore and it is certainly not the solution to disrupting other industries that need it. (BLC) potential is being identified as something that can solve problems beyond just currency, and the manifestation of that value is going into the Altcoin space for those coins that are looking to do just that.

Always remember that we're in a high-risk space, with tremendous volatility. However, if you believe in it, and believe it is a disruptive force for the betterment of humankind (and our wallets), then we have to ride these downturns. If we believe there is a future in Crypto, then the tides will turn again and we'll move back up, so there is nothing to worry about, since we're all in it for the long haul.

Knowledge—Lack of it will be the One Problem that Holds You Back

Now that you have a better understanding of the history of the Worldwide Digital Coins and why they exist, it's time to examine if you want to invest in the market, sit on the sidelines waiting, or just be a knowledgeable individual that wants to just keep up with the world and where it's going with digital currencies.

As we move forward in your education of this fascinating world of digital coins, we will be asking ourselves many questions, and the answers to those questions will determine where you stand on your involvement.

PART 2:

HOW TO GET STARTED

How Much Money Can I Afford to Lose?

Well, if you're still ready, you must be anxious and excited to learn more about how to get involved. Getting involved can cost an investment of as little as $100 to as much as any individual can afford to lose.

We are at the beginning of what will make everyone forget how big cell phones and the Internet were. Anybody that starts to get involved in 2018 will be positioned to make as much money as you want depending on your investment.

2018 will be the year of the Altcoins making their way into mainstream for advanced applications in every industry. Making smart, informed decisions with a team of advisors for your investments into the strongest Altcoins that become available will have better returns than a successful penny stock back in the day!

Please remember with any investment that you might choose there are never any guarantees. But there are also many opportunities to make a fortune! The best time for an investment is always upon the inception of something that will last.

Making well-informed Altcoin investments can turn into one of the most profitable times in our world as we know it.

So, again, we say you need to be comfortable with

"How Much Money Can You Afford to Lose?"

Have your Eyes, Ears, and Mind

Open to the Abundance of Opportunities to

Invest in well-positioned companies with Altcoins!

How Much Money Do I Want to Make?

The amount of money you want to invest will be determined as we discussed in the last chapter. How much money can we afford to lose? That's really not the plan B. We always need to be prepared for the worst in such a volatile new market. What we call the *"New Asset Class."*

Money is always relative to the person hold the funds. Investing $500 can mean the same to another person that invests $5,000 or $50,000. So once the decision is made on "How Much," we need to allocate the funds to two portfolios.

Now that we have decided how much money to put into digital coins, the question that needs to be answered is: "How do I allocate my investment funds?"

We will set up two types of portfolios based on the investment amount you decide to start with. The first is the "Core." The second is the "Opportunity—Speculative." In addition, we will have a "Coins of Interest" group that we will constantly monitor and continue to research before we decide to invest. We will call this our ***"Investment Funnel."***

The Core Portfolio

This is where we will put 80% of our funds. Example: if we have $5,000, this portfolio will have approximately $4,000 of Blue Chip coins. My personal core portfolio as of February 7, 2018, is shown below.

Name	Symbol	Portfolio %	Current Price	Market Cap	% Chg since 12/1/2017
Bitcoin	BTC	43%	$9,546.97	$161,192,473,526.00	-13.016%
Ethereum	ETH	15%	$818.55	$80,071,257,867.00	75.451%
Monero	XMR	10%	$265.23	$4,179,724,542.00	38.908%
Litecoin	LTC	10%	$198.97	$11,016,032,332.00	100.983%
NEO	NEO	5%	$114.50	$7,442,435,000.00	219.473%
Zcash	ZEC	5%	$380.54	$1,275,105,758.00	13.262%
Stellar	XLM	4%	$0.35	$6,402,611,612.00	285.713%
Cardano	ADA	4%	$0.32	$8,235,319,123.00	141.819%
EOS	EOS	4%	$7.97	$5,505,976,817.00	146.125%

The core portfolio is our bedrock. Every pick here is one we intend to hold for the long term. They're based on hardcore fundamentals, research, and—most importantly—what the best investors in our network are holding.

Our top hedge fund friends and our group of investors are holding most of these as well.

If there are material changes to any crypto in the core portfolio, we'll be ahead of the curve and our group knowledge is shared among the group to make intelligent decisions for buying and selling. It's primarily long term but always monitoring.

A prime example of this was with Litecoin (LTC). Our group made the decision to purchase Litecoin with a 15% stake for our Core Portfolio in early November 2017 when it was selling for $55. At the time, we were thinking a long-term play. Right after our January 4, 2018, group meeting, we felt it was overvalued and decided to sell out of it at $266 dollars and take the huge profits.

Then we put it back in our investment funnel while we keep an eye on it. We anticipate the new LitePay Credit Card will bring strong value back in a huge way and the group should be moving it back into our core.

With your core, you will have a basket of cryptos with a solid foundation. You could go to sleep … and wake up five years later and odds are high that this portfolio alone will have created wealth.

The Speculative-Opportunity Portfolio

This portfolio will use the remaining, or 20% of your funds. Again, all coins are constantly monitored throughout the group. In this group, we will be looking for big spikes and dips with parameters in place to buy and sell. These coins can also be moved into the core based on company developments that would make them a long-term play. In addition, this one has a "Buy Up To" column in which you will be able to see some results depending on when you got the book. My personal Speculative Portfolio as of February 7, 2018, is shown below.

Name	Symbol	Portfolio %	Current Price	Market Cap	% Chg since 12/1/2017	Buy Up To
OmiseGO	OMG	2%	$16.64	$1,697,681,934.00	103.635%	$25.00
Steem	STEEM	2%	$3.40	$850,307,538.00	243.012%	$10.00
SALT	SALT	2%	$4.51	$242,483,049.00	7.03%	$12.00
Genesis Vision	GVT	1%	$20.33	$75,765,828.00	185.535%	$20.00
Binance Coin	BNB	2%	$8.80	$871,778,664.00	325.343%	$15.00
Metal	MTL	2%	$3.88	$74,862,572.00	-26.12%	$6.00
Ark	ARK	2%	$3.53	$356,311,313.00	2.707%	$8.00
Time New Bank	TNB	2%	$0.05	$89,241,420.00	100.678%	$0.40
WAX	WAX	1%	$0.29	$141,563,726.00	N/A	$2.00
Particl	PART	1%	$21.93	$194,728,262.00	172.048%	$30.00
VeChain	VEN	2%	$5.42	$2,586,713,583.00	1535.793%	$6.50
0x	ZRX	1%	$0.88	$453,510,250.00	337.514%	$2.00

An example that we had in this group was Ripple (XRP). All of our indicators put us in a position to buy in at the beginning of December for 48 cents. The Board of Investors was voted in unanimously on December 30, 2017, right before New Year's Eve to sell out for $2.48. Another huge profit and win!

Coins of Interest in the Funnel

The coins in this portfolio are ones that meet all our criteria and show up on our radar to be listed in this portfolio. But we don't feel that they are mature enough—or have enough potential yet—to be part of the core portfolio.

This is where you'll find Altcoins that can rise fast in a year or two and even in days or weeks. So, don't be surprised to make significant returns from this portfolio in that period.

Unlike our core portfolio, we're more likely to liquidate our coins here to take profits from time to time.

Plus, this is a growing list that we will add to regularly. So, we don't advise how to allocate your investment dollars to these.

Of course, while there's no "official" allocation in this portfolio … here's what you *could* do.

For the purposes of this allocation, think of investing in terms of (BC). Remember, it is currently the standard currency that most (CC) are bought and traded in.

With that in mind, you can take a (BC) and split it into quarters.

Each time I send out a buy alert for the opportunity portfolio, you could buy a quarter of a (BC) worth in that (CC).

You can do this with a fraction of a (BC) or multiple (BC). Just divide whatever (BC) amount you start with, into quarters and invest that quarter in each new buy alert.

I like investing this way. It's simple.

You shouldn't also worry about the price of (BC) at the time. That's already been baked into the research we do for buy alerts.

As always, we are monitoring and researching for news alerts and waiting for all the parameters to kick in to indicate the time to buy.

A good example for this group is Time New Bank (TNB). Again, the coin meets all the requirements for the Board to make a decision to buy.

This one showed up at the beginning of December 2017 when all the stars aligned for the Board to give the green light to purchase. The buy-in decision was made at 25 cents and we used 2% of our funds to invest. On this one we got a little greedy and we should have sold in the beginning of January 2018 for $3.73, but we hung on until January the 12th and sold out for $2.02. We took the profit and felt there were some negative indicators, so we took it out of our coins of interest portfolio and moved them into the Research & Development Department (R&D). On February 6, we bought back in for 4.5 cents and have moved them into the Speculative Portfolio.

The Altcoins that are in (R&D) are all in our Crypto Funnel and we are waiting to move the worthy ones to Coins of Interest.

The following projects are closely monitored but they haven't yet been added to the portfolio. Our Coins of Interest list is also where we may keep coins that we've taken profits on or moved out of the portfolio if we still like the project long term.

Here's our Coins of interest Personal Funnel at this time:

Name	Symbol	Portfolio %	Current Price	Market Cap	% Chg since 12/1/2017
Counterparty	XCP	0%	$22.93	$60,021,251.00	5.979%
Cindicator	CND	0%	$0.14	$198,869,498.00	531.175%
Ardor	ARDR	0%	$0.41	$410,758,622.00	17.779%
Dragonchain	DRGN	0%	$1.35	$321,213,959.00	N/A
Aion	AION	0%	$2.89	$278,018,628.00	86.541%
Shift	SHIFT	0%	$2.69	$31,631,478.00	20.67%

Altcoin Analysis—How to Pick Them?

Now we can get into the plan and the basic strategy that the Board uses to determine when we get in our out of a specific coin.

There are three main factors we use when making decisions on new ICO and existing Altcoins. The chart below shows us the three main points for a particular coin that needs to be met just to get in the coin funnel whether in (R&D), Coins of Interest, Speculative, or the main Core Portfolio.

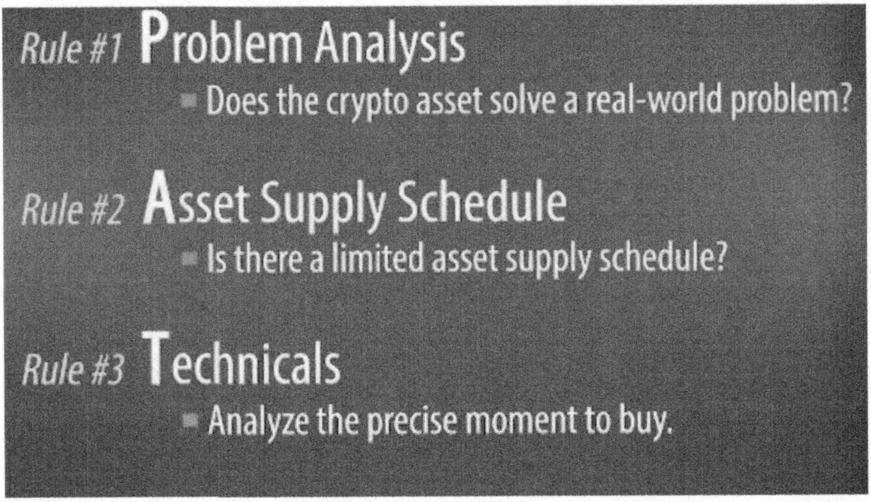

Let's start with Rule #1: Problem Analysis.

Who are the clients the (BLC) will serve and what real-world problem and pain will it solve for those customers? How does the target customer try to solve that problem and pain currently? What are the *"Benefits"* of the Altcoin Blockchain and Smart Contracts that will help them solve the problems of the current applications that are in place? Plus, what are the *"Benefits of the Benefits?"* This always adds up for the company to have more time for other areas of the business and that equates to more money and profits.

Rule #2: Asset Supply Schedule

Whenever looking at a particular Altcoin, you have to look at what or if there is a limit on the coins. Any coin that does not have a limit needs to be taken off the list immediately. It is as simple as seventh-grade economics. Which is Supply & Demand. The coins that have the ability to make more coins are pretty much "Money Grab Scams!"

With a limit, there will never be anymore and as the company grows and prospers there are way more buyers than coins which then makes the price go up.

Just like stocks the only way for more stock of a company is a "split." In Altcoins, it's a "fork" and in layman terms, you double your money.

For example (BC) has only 21 million coins and the demand got so insane the price went all the way to $20,000 per coin, so crazy, right?

Rule #3: Technicals

This is the most precise of the three and where the real work comes in. One man alone just can't do it alone!

With approximately 3,000 Altcoins out there and 10–15 new ones per day you need a well-educated team behind you to handle the (R&D) so you make the decisions at the right moment when all the "technicals" line up.

Lastly, 95% of them fail and you want to make sure you don't get involved with those.

All of this requires large amounts of research time with information forwarded to the main team to be processed before a decision can be made to buy and sell.

As a reader of this book you will be entitled to a free month on our Platinum Service with no obligation financially on your part. This will be explained at the back of the book.

The next two charts will show the cycles of assets of how they grow and evolve. This chart applies to all the major assets that are traded. Stocks, Gold, Bonds, Commodities, etc. The cycle is always the same for growing stable assets.

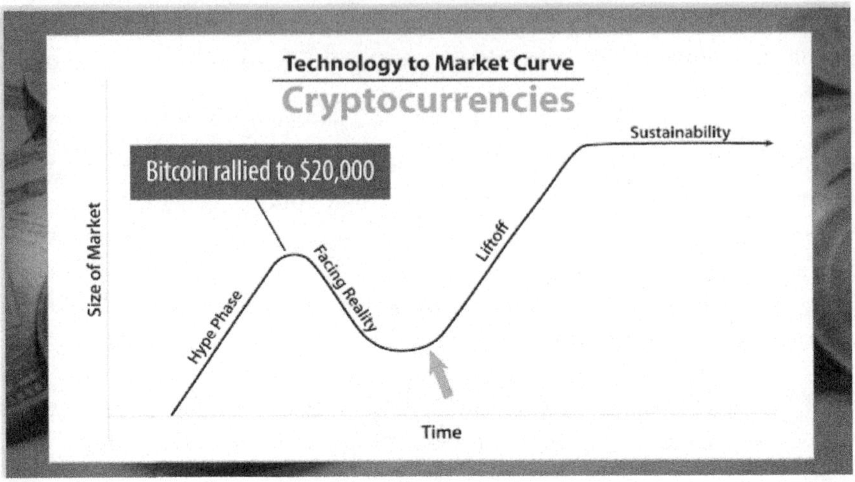

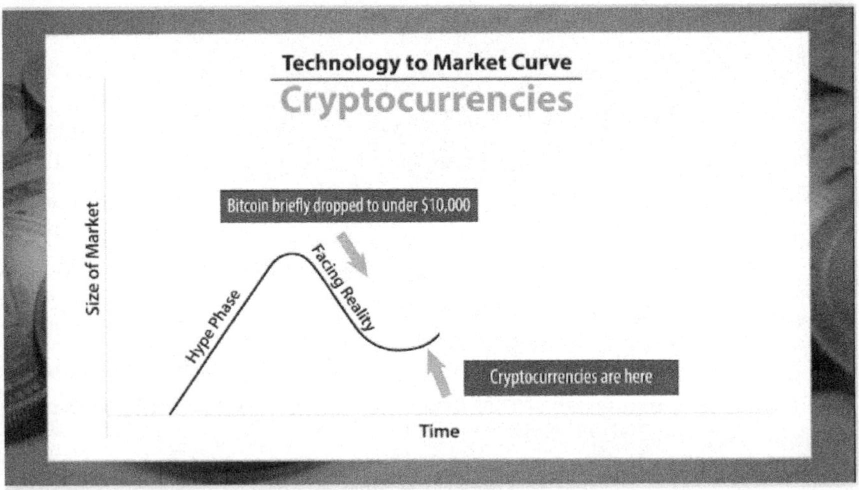

<u>Here we go back to the question:</u>

"Is it too late to get in the game?"

The answer is "Hell No!"

BITCOIN IS JUST THE BEGINNING!

IT'S NOT TOO LATE TO START INVESTING AND TRADING IN ALTCOINS

Maybe you're still thinking that it might be too late to get into Bitcoin and (CC)?—it's not. (BC) and its underlying (BLC) technology are revolutionary, and possibilities have just barely begun to be realized.

That's the opportunity for us.

Let's review. We now have learned about the history of this new asset class and what we can now call "The Future of Finance" that utilizes the (BLC) technology.

We now have a better understanding of Bitcoin, digital crypto currencies, and Altcoins. The good, the bad, and the ugly.

The innovations to come in the next few years will make perfect sense to you, when it leaves people in the mainstream flabbergasted as they try to figure it out, as Altcoins begin to enter their lives whether they are ready for it or not.

Next, we decided how much money we can afford to lose and how much money we want to make. Let's take our investment amount of $500—$5,000—$50,000 and see what some realistic numbers can be with a great team making the intelligent decisions, to make anywhere from 200% to 5,000% or even more.

I'll use the $5,000 investment and let's say I want to make 200% on my money. That means your profit margin is $10,000 If its 1000% it turns into $50,000 profit.

Now that we know how much we can afford to lose (Not Happening) what we want to make, let's go make some money!

But How Do We Get Our Dollars into Altcoins?

The essentials to start building your future in (CC) can be challenging. Now that you have some insight into how all this started, we shed some more light on the subject to make this journey easier for all involved. The media will give you only bits and pieces of information, just enough to arouse your interest, but not enough to really help you understand what is really going on.

It doesn't have to be that way. We can help shed some light on the subject.

It should be as simple as just going to a website and buying some of the coins you want. But it's just not that easy. Interactions between users, merchants, exchanges, and platforms can be a little clunky or technical at times. The crypto ecosystem is not really user-friendly yet. It's not designed for the mainstream.

That shouldn't turn you off though, that should get you excited. As you see the amount of money going into the space right now, and you realize that it still isn't mainstream, then you'll understand how huge the potential is.

It's like getting your first e-mail address in 1994, when the user experience wasn't quite worked out yet. But how's that Internet thing doing? Pretty good, right? Similar process happening here.

We're going to show you the easiest way to get started buying and using (CC).

In this section, we will learn how to:

How to begin buying Altcoins—you don't have to be an expert trader, banker, or financial wizard to participate in this movement. Anyone can do this!

What you need to do to keep your coins secure—one of the fundamental features of (CC) is autonomy. You have control of your money rather than a bank, brokerage, or government. Our most important objective is to help you be as informed and educated about (CC) as possible.

Set up a wallet—it is still surprising how easy it is to set up crypto accounts and wallets versus running the gauntlet at a bank or traditional financial service institution.

Wallets

In this section, we're going to talk about the different kinds of digital wallets where you can keep your coins once you get them. Later, we'll walk you through installing a wallet on your computer and show you how to use it. This is just a general overview of the kinds of crypto wallets that are out there. Get familiar with these types so you can assess your own situation and decide what wallets work best for you.

When you initially get some Bitcoin, or any other coin, asset, or token, you will need to keep it in a digital wallet. As a rule of thumb, wallets are designed for specific coins. For example, you keep Bitcoin in a Bitcoin wallet. You keep Ethereum in an Ethereum wallet. Essentially, there is at least one wallet for each and every coin. But there are increasingly more options for the more popular coins and there are also multi-coin and multi-asset wallets.

To help keep things as simple as possible for you, we are recommending a multi-asset wallet that can hold several of the most popular coins and assets. I'll walk you through setting up that wallet in just a bit.

It's going to seem like there are a lot of different kinds of wallets and at first, you might find this section a little confusing. Don't worry. I'm going to break down the different kinds of wallets into simple categories. It's important to know these distinctions, so don't let this section overwhelm you.

Keep in mind that it's common for someone to have several different wallets, even if you only had one coin such as (BC).

Hot and Cold Wallets

One basic distinction is the difference between a "hot wallet" and a "cold wallet." A hot wallet is one that you expect to access often, using it to send money or buy things. It is used on a device that has easy Internet access. Hot wallets are more vulnerable because they are more accessible, and because you tend to use them more often and in different environments.

Think of your hot wallet like the cash you might keep in your pocket. For security reasons, it is best not to keep a lot of money in this kind of wallet.

A cold wallet is generally kept offline. Cold wallets are therefore more secure. It follows that it is best to keep most of your coins in a cold wallet rather than a hot wallet. When you know you'll need to access those coins, you can move them to a hot wallet or make the transaction directly. But generally, cold wallets are less accessible by design.

In sum, if the hot wallet is used to store the cash in your pocket, then, by analogy, a cold wallet is akin to storing large amounts of cash in a safe in your house. You can still get at it relatively quickly, but you don't take it shopping with you.

Desktop, Online or Web, Mobile, Hardware

Desktop:

This is simply a wallet installed on a computer. You will need access to the Internet, but you can also manage your coins offline. Generally speaking, a desktop wallet is the best compromise between security and practical use. The Exodus wallet that we will be using is a desktop wallet.

Online:

An online or web wallet keeps your coins stored in the cloud with a third-party provider. It is convenient, as you can access them from any device. But, of course, it is less secure depending on how you access it and because of the fact that you must rely on a third party to secure your money.

Mobile:

A mobile wallet is one that you keep on your smartphone, tablet, or another mobile device. They often use QR codes to make transactions. Mobile wallets are convenient but not recommended for long-term storage. It is less secure to keep coins on a mobile device.

Hardware:

This is the most secure option. You will have to pay for your hardware wallet while most other wallets are free, but as far as security goes, this is about as good as you can get. They're great for storage and easy to take with you, similar to an external hard drive. You can connect this wallet to a computer and transact online, then disconnect it again to keep it secure. The Ledger Nano works with the most exchanges & Trezor is the second-most exchange hardware wallet that we are recommending. As you get more involved, it will probably be best to have both.

I mentioned earlier that people commonly use several different wallets depending on their needs. We recommend a desktop wallet, an online hot wallet, and a hardware wallet as a basic suite of wallets that can cover all your needs. If you do not intend to keep a large amount of money in coins, a hardware wallet like the Ledger Nano & Trezor may be unnecessary. You will have to determine how much you will be investing in (CC) and how you will keep them.

The Exodus desktop will be the simplest and most secure without getting any new hardware. So, let's start with it. To give you a better idea of how it all works, let's walk through the setup and security of Exodus, our desktop wallet recommendation.

Exodus Installation Walkthrough

The Exodus desktop wallet is free, easy to install, secure, fast, and it looks pretty sharp. It is a multi-asset wallet that supports the most popular coins such as Bitcoin, Ethereum, and Litecoin, as well as a number of other crypto assets such as OmiseGo and Civic. It also has a built-in exchange which you can use to swap coins and diversify your portfolio without having to use an exchange. It's not really for trading, however, as the fees are not as competitive as actual exchanges, but it is an excellent feature for the sake of convenience.

I'm going to walk you through installing Exodus on your computer. Go to the Exodus wallet main page.

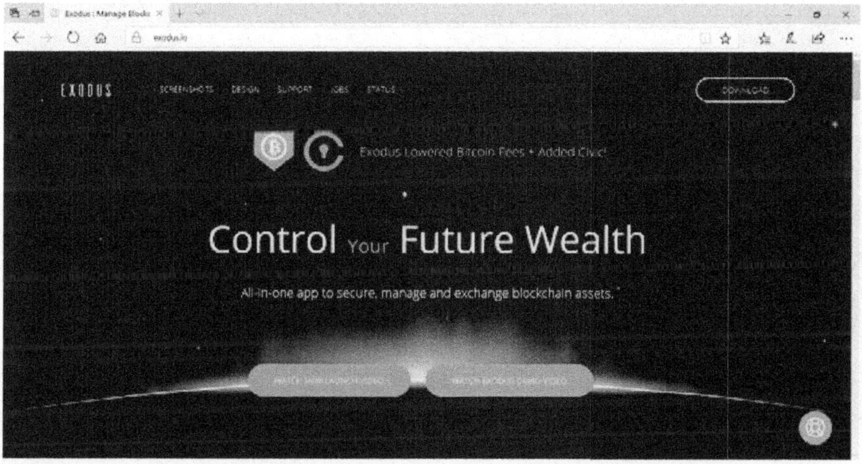

Click on the Download button on the top right. You will then see the choices for the type of operating system you have. Choose your operating system.

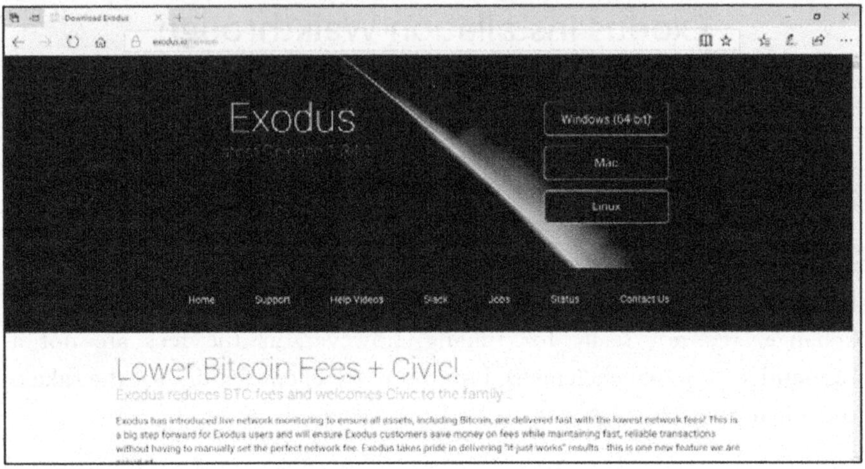

You will see a pop-up at the bottom. You can Save the installation application on your computer and then double-click it to begin installation, or you can just click on Run and it will begin installing.

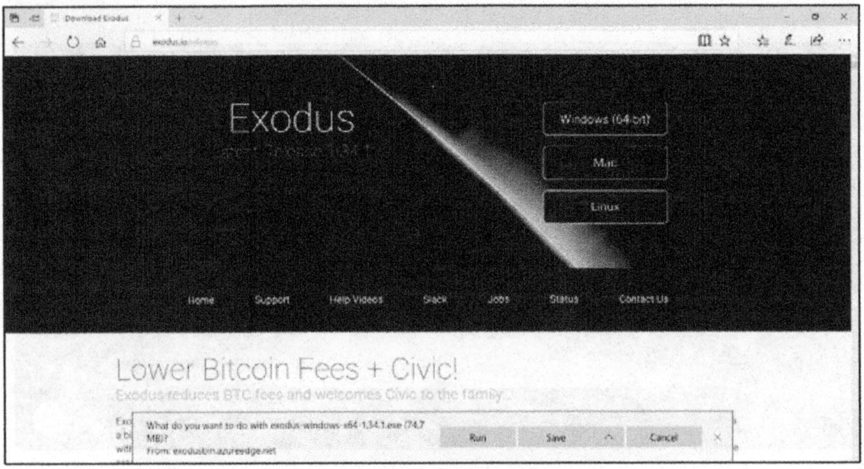

You should see this pop-up as it installs.

The wallet application should run as soon as it completes installation. If not, you should see an Exodus icon on your desktop. Double-click that to run it for the first time. If you need help or have any questions, the Exodus website has a great help section with many videos showing you how to install or use the wallet.

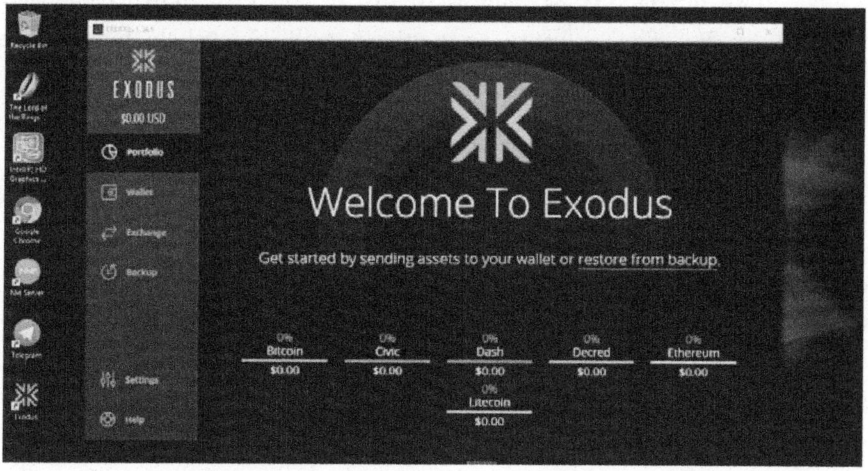

Congratulations! You now have your first crypto wallet!

Before we begin putting coins into that wallet, let's talk first about an important security point.

A big question people always ask is—"what if my computer hard drive crashes? Are my (BC) gone?"

Well, yes and no. All wallets have a backup feature, and different kinds of backups. You should use them all. If you back up your wallet, you can recover any lost coins.

How?

Look at it this way. Your wallet is your access to your (BC) on the (BLC). If your computer crashes, your (BC) are still there on the (BLC). As long as the (BLC) still exists on some other computer somewhere in the world (and it always will), your (BC) are still there.

What you've lost is your key to those (BC). If you've backed up your wallet and copied and written down your passwords, passphrases, or private key, you can reconstruct your wallet and regain access to your coins.

"What if I didn't back up my wallet? What happens to those coins?"

Well, you wouldn't be the first.

It's estimated that as many as 10% of all (BC) created may have been "lost" in this way. They still exist, sitting there on the blockchain, but nobody knows the key to retrieve them.

And because they are secured cryptographically, it will be a long time before they can be accessed. If ever.

If you have a desktop wallet, anything that jeopardizes your computer (theft, malware, mechanical problem, hard drive failure) could restrict your access to your own wallet. Always back up your wallet, in multiple ways if possible. Your wallet isn't your coins, your wallet is what gives you easy and secure access to them. Lose your wallet and you lose your access. Your coins are still on the (BLC).

If you lose a wallet with cash in it, your money is gone. But you can back up your crypto wallet and reconstruct it if you are prepared.

You will read the horror stories of people losing computers, leaving them in the cafeteria at a (BC) convention, having hard drive failures without backing up, or reformatting a hard drive and erasing the key to $25,000 in Bitcoin.

Learn from their mistakes.

Backing Up Your Exodus Wallet:

You can see that the Exodus wallet developers take wallet backup seriously—they've made it one of the main tabs on the screen. In the example below you can see there are already a few coins in the wallet. And there is a red warning sign on that Backup tab.

We need to back up this wallet now so we don't lose access to our coins in case something happens to this computer. You haven't put any coins into your wallet yet, but go ahead and back up your wallet as we go through this walkthrough.

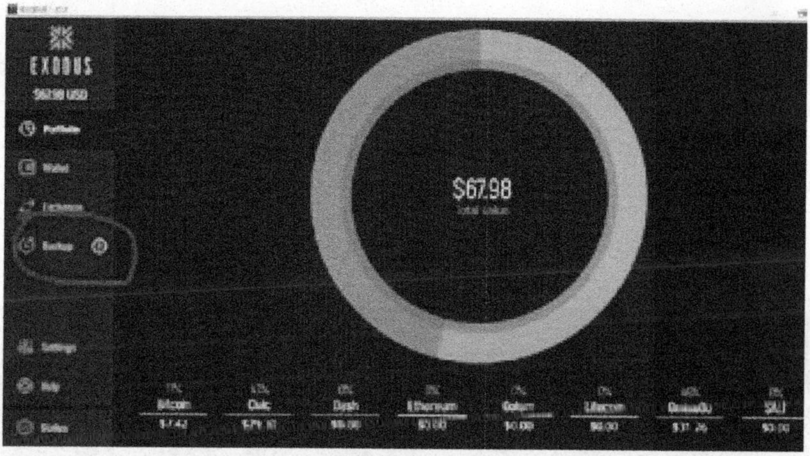

Click on the Backup tab on the left side. This will start a simple four-step process to back up your wallet. The first step is to create a password.

Step 2 simply asks you to check your password again. The Exodus developers take your security very seriously. They won't even let you make a mistake on your own password!

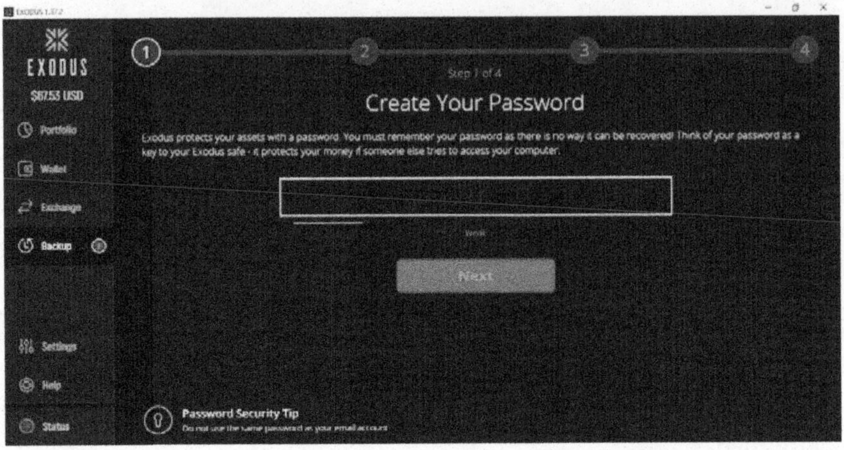

Now, step 3 is kind of interesting. Here, it's giving you your recovery passphrase. This is common with crypto applications. Print this out or write it down somewhere, it's very important. This will allow you to reconstruct your wallet and restore your assets, should something happen.

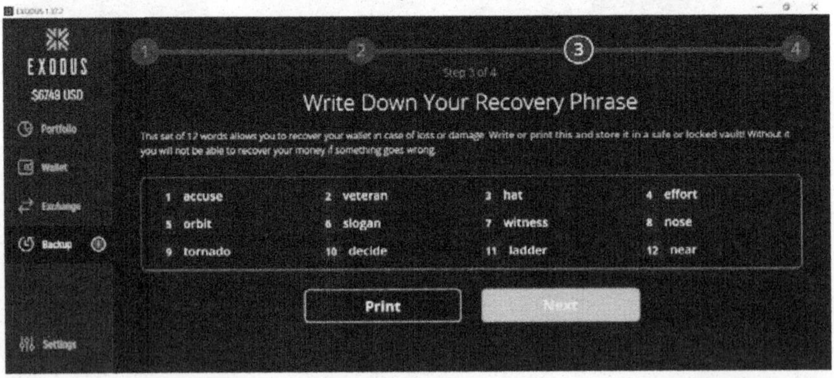

The last step is to provide an e-mail address for a backup link.

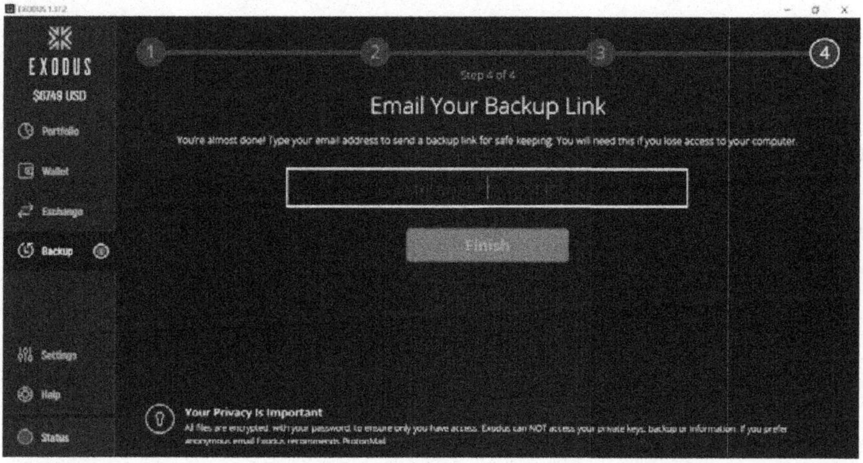

That's it! A simple four-step process that provides several ways to secure your coins. You can now start funding your wallet with some confidence.

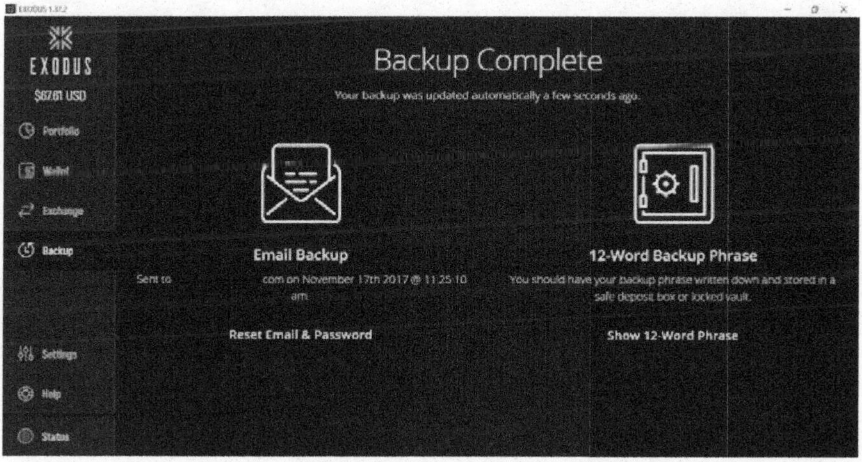

Crypto Exchanges—Which Ones are Best

Coinbase is the number one exchange in the world as we speak, and Binance is #2. Coinbase has Bitcoin, Bitcoin Cash, Ethereum, and Litecoin. Binance has the largest number of successful coins and is very stringent in its policy on bringing in new Altcoins.

So, let's show you how to get started in Coinbase Registration.

Coinbase Registration Walkthrough:

Now you are going to open a Coinbase account. Go to the Coinbase homepage. Click on the Sign-Up button which you can see on the top right.

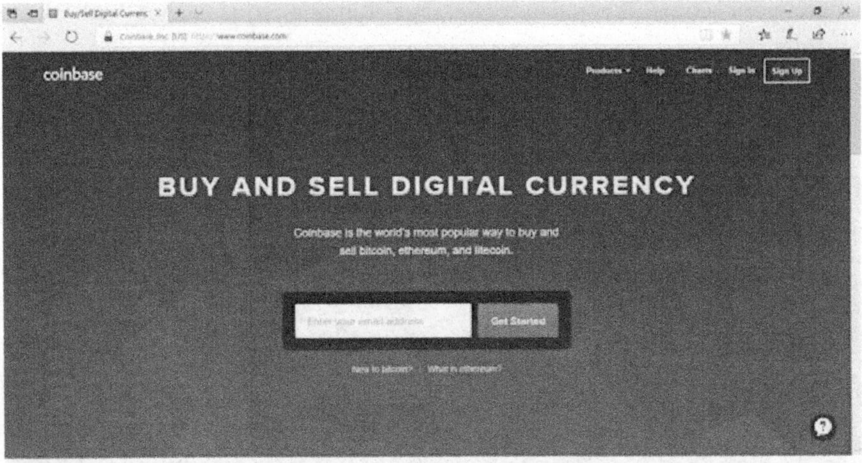

You'll need to input the information they ask for, fill the captcha, and click Create Account.

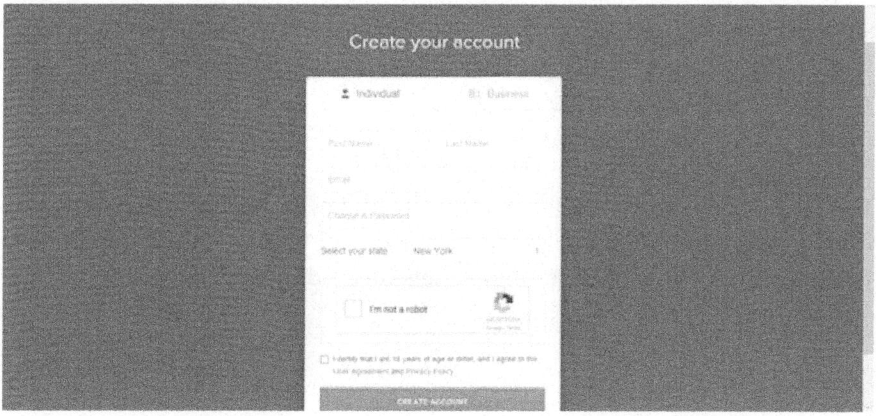

The first page you see is the dashboard with the prices of Bitcoin, Ethereum, and Litecoin.

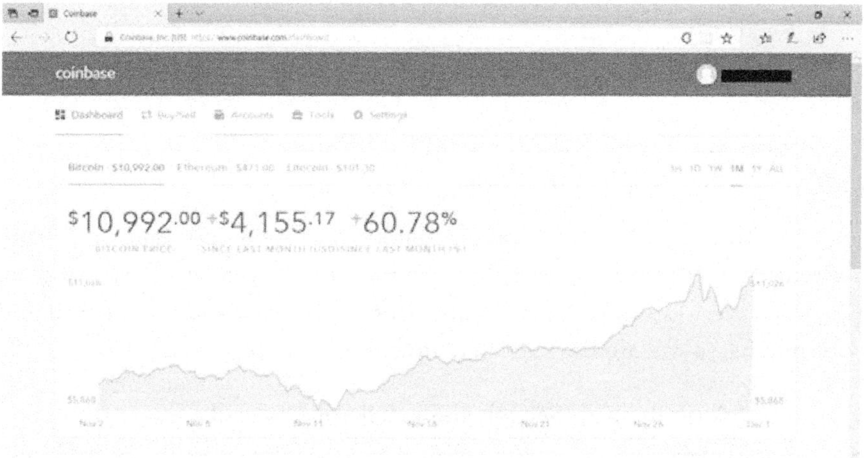

If you scroll down that page a bit, you will see a progress bar on the left side with your account creation information. They're asking you to add your phone number for 2-Factor authorization, an extra level of security. After you have done this, when you sign in, they will send you a text with a code number. You will need to have your phone with you to receive that code and get into your account. 2- Factor Authorization, or 2FA, is a security feature that is quite common today for websites or accounts that deal with personal assets.

Once you have your account established, you will have the option to use a third-party security application such as Google Authenticator or Authy. These applications are more secure than a text message so it's recommended that you change your 2FA settings to this method.

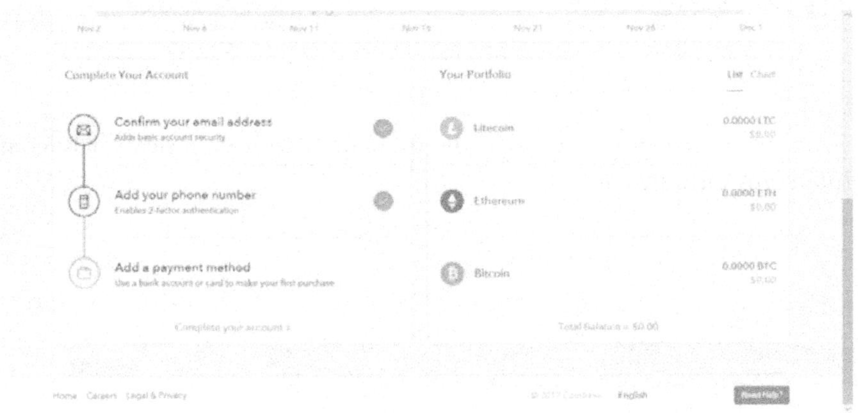

Coinbase will then require additional information to link your bank account or credit card. Once you do that, you'll be able to buy Bitcoin, Ethereum, and Litecoin directly from your bank account or credit card and your purchases will appear right here in your Coinbase account.

Click on the Buy/Sell tab and you'll see a page like this.

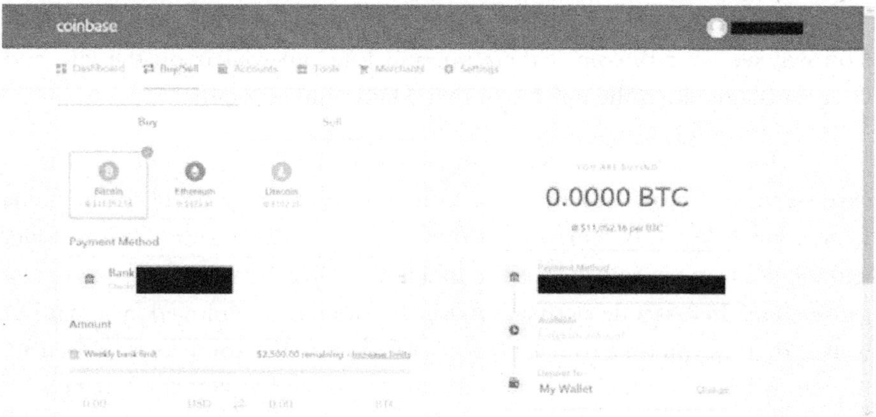

You can see the "Buy" tab is highlighted by default and the Bitcoin icon is checked. Scroll down just a bit and you'll see that your payment method is already set. You can fill in a dollar amount or an amount of Bitcoin that you want to buy and click on the buy button to initiate the purchase.

And that's it—a one-click purchase of Bitcoin!

If you wanted to buy Litecoin instead, just click on the tab at the top and you will see Litecoin with a green check and the button at the bottom will read "Buy Litecoin."

After making a purchase, click on the Accounts tab on the top line. You will see your Bitcoin, Ethereum, and Litecoin wallets on the left, and your transactions on the right with their status and amounts.

On the above screen, on the left you can see My Vault. That is an extra security feature of Coinbase. You can move some or all of the coins from your wallet into your vault. Consider your wallet more of a hot wallet and the coins in your vault as more of a cold wallet. If you want to withdraw those coins there is a delay of a few days before they are moved into that hot wallet. It gives you time to react if you or Coinbase has some kind of security breach. It's an extra feature that most exchanges and wallets don't have.

Some people are comfortable with trusting Coinbase and prefer to leave their coins there for convenience. Others prefer the freedom of having control of their own wallet. Of course, you can do both—leave some in Coinbase and keep some in other wallets.

It is always recommended to diversify—both the types of your assets and where you keep your funds.

Funding Your Wallet

Now we are going to look at a critical process for trading crypto—moving assets between exchanges, wallets, and merchants. Pay close attention because this is a very different process from what most people are familiar with.

We will start by moving some Bitcoin from our Coinbase account to our Exodus wallet.

Open your Exodus wallet and click on the Wallet tab on the left. Make sure you have Bitcoin selected. You can see it is a different color than the other coins and the Bitcoin icon is at the top center of the screen. This way you know for sure that you are sending or receiving Bitcoins.

This screen shows you how much Bitcoin is currently in your wallet and gives you a list of your most recent transactions.

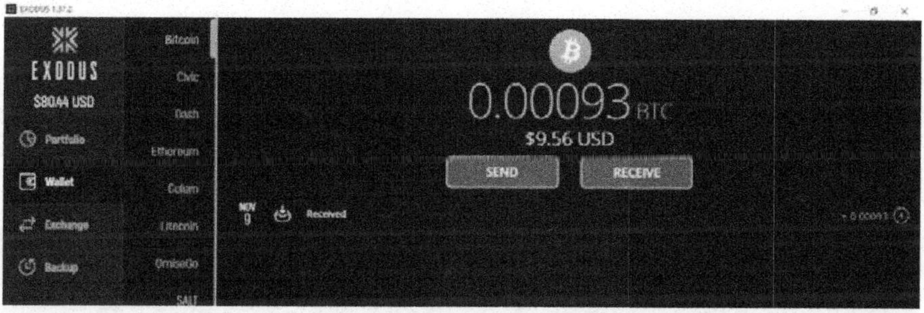

Click on the Receive button and you will see a pop-up. What's you're seeing in this picture are some of the basic features of cryptocurrencies that you need to get familiar with.

There is a QR code, that's the box with the random jumble of squares in it. You've likely already seen these around. You can scan that code as the receiving address for Bitcoins in your wallet with a variety of applications, but we won't be using that right now.

For now, pay attention to what's happening just below that. Your Bitcoin address for your Exodus wallet is displayed—it's that long, seemingly random jumble of letters and numbers. That's what crypto addresses look like.

Look at the icons beneath your address. The one on the left is to copy and paste the address to your clipboard. If you hover your cursor over each symbol for a second, it will tell you what each icon is for.

Click on that and your address is now copied to your clipboard.

That's the address that you will be sending Bitcoins to from Coinbase.

Now, go ahead and sign in to your Coinbase account.

Once you are in, click on the accounts tab.

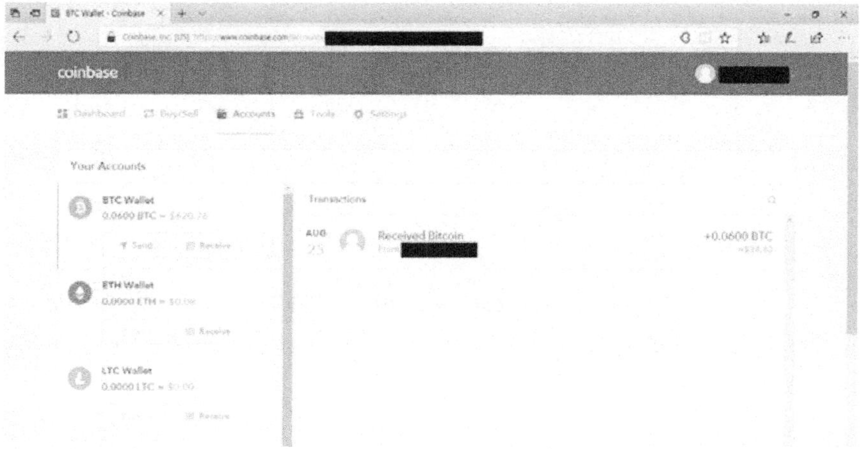

In this example account, we can see the Bitcoin wallet on the left with 0.0600 Bitcoin, and the current Dollar value. On the right, we can see the only transaction for this account. It received that 0.0600 BTC on August 25, 2016.

We are going to send that balance of 0.0600 Bitcoins to our Exodus wallet.

You can see two buttons underneath the Bitcoin wallet: Send and Receive. Since we want to send these Bitcoins, click on the Send button and you will see a pop-up.

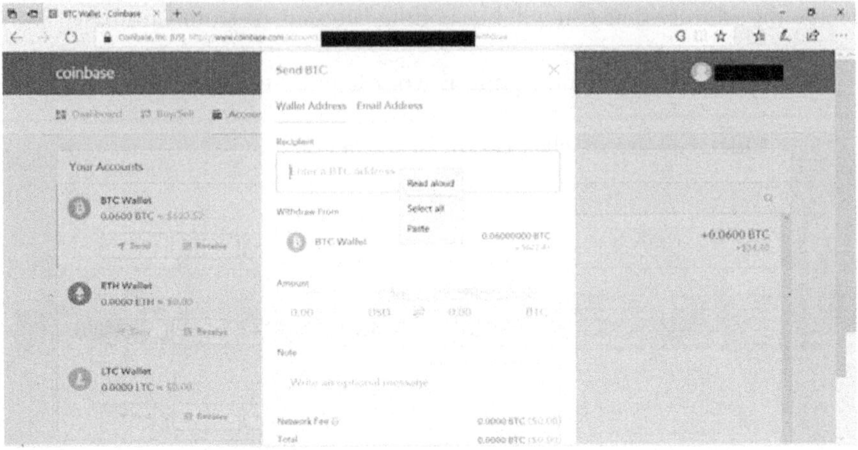

In this pop-up, you can see that "Wallet Address" is already highlighted. The other option is Email Address, but this time we are sending directly to a wallet.

Remember that we already copied our wallet address to our clipboard. This way, we won't have to try to type out all of those upper-case and lower-case letters and numbers. Click inside the recipient box to enter your Exodus wallet address. With your cursor in that box, right click and you will see the Paste option as in the picture. Select that and you should see your Exodus wallet address populate that box like in the picture below.

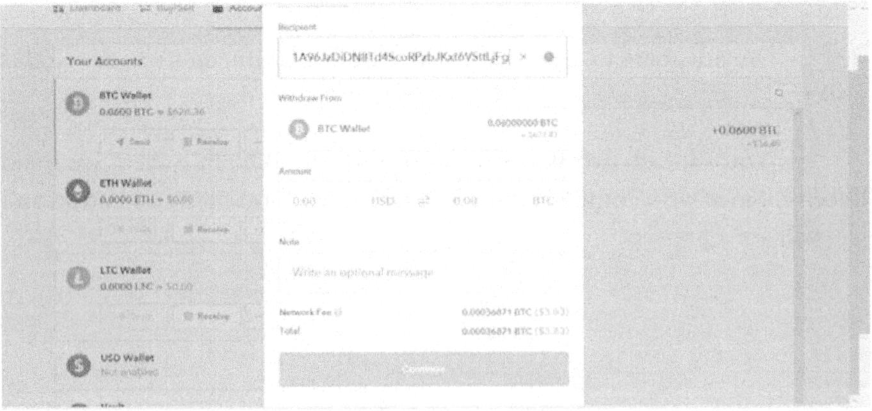

I always double-check the address. I make sure to look at the first and last few letters just to make sure something wasn't cut off or lost in the copy/paste process. You may want to go back and look at the open window on your Exodus wallet to confirm the address. Some addresses are even longer than this one and you may have to scroll in the window to the beginning of the box and to the end to see it all.

I have not yet had a problem with copy/paste not properly filling an address in a field, but we're talking about something with real value here. It's best to be careful until you're totally comfortable.

And just to ease some of your fears with this process—if some of the address does get cut off, or entered incorrectly, it will most likely cause the transaction to fail with no coins being moved. It's technically not impossible to make a mistake and send your coins to an unintended recipient, but it's pretty difficult. Just be cautious and you'll be OK.

Further down in the pop-up you can see that you need to input the amount you're sending. You can set it in dollars or Bitcoins. In this case, we're sending the maximum amount.

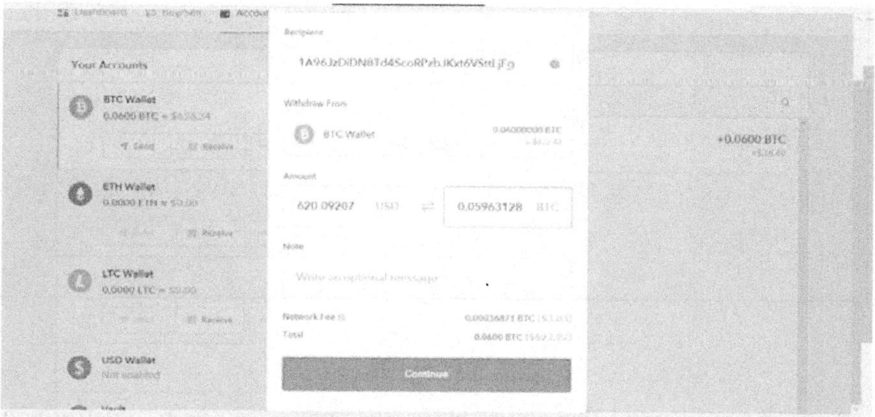

You can see that the maximum amount we're sending is actually a bit less than 0.06 BTC. That's because of the transaction fee (or network fee as it's called here), which you can see on the bottom. That's the fee in Bitcoins that goes to the computers that are running the Bitcoin blockchain network.

When you are satisfied that everything is in order, the only thing left to do is to click the "Continue" button and send those Bitcoins from your Coinbase account to your Exodus wallet.

This moment can be exhilarating and terrifying at the same time. Will it actually work? Will those Bitcoins appear in my wallet or did I just send my money out into cyberspace?

If there is a problem, you will most likely immediately see an error saying the transaction failed, "incorrect address," or something to that effect. You can then fix it and resend.

But it should go through just fine, and you will see the transaction recorded with the amount and status as in the picture below.

Keep in mind that, most likely, the transaction won't go through immediately. Blockchain-based transactions require confirmations from the network which takes time. It could process very quickly or it may take several minutes. Don't panic. If you really want to watch it happen, keep your Coinbase account open and your wallet open and check them for status updates.

When complete, you will see your portfolio in your Exodus wallet updated with the new funds.

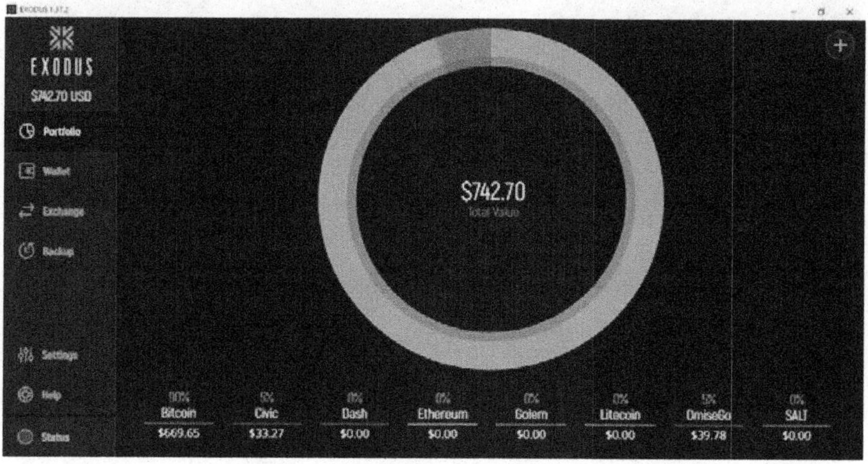

Making an Exchange in Exodus

Now that you have some funds in your wallet, let's look at something a little different.

The Exodus wallet has a special feature that lets you exchange between the coins that the wallet supports. That means that your wallet can act like its very own crypto-exchange. Compared to a full exchange you'll pay higher fees and have less functionality, but having this feature within your own personal wallet can be really helpful with lesser amounts.

Let's take a look at how an exchange in Exodus works in case you like some of the coins it supports and the convenience of just exchanging a little in your wallet.

Keep an eye on the total value of the portfolio below. Not only will you see it updated regularly as coin values change, you'll see what happens to it during this coin exchange.

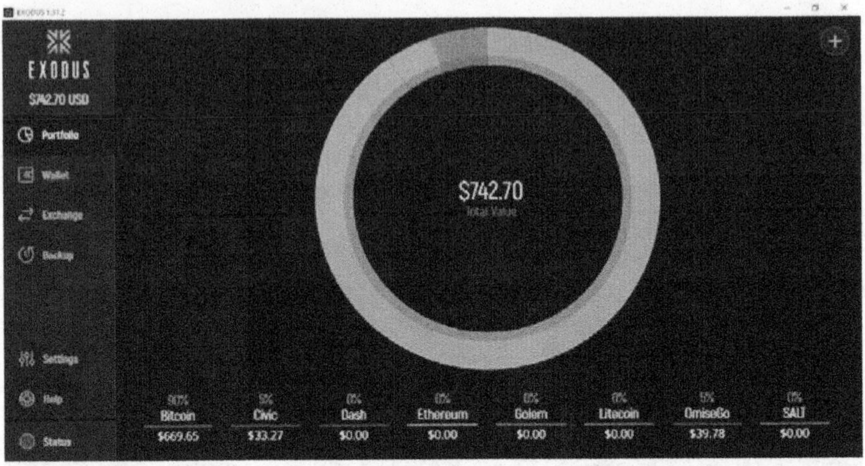

In your own wallet, click on the Exchange tab just under the Portfolio tab so you can see what this looks like.

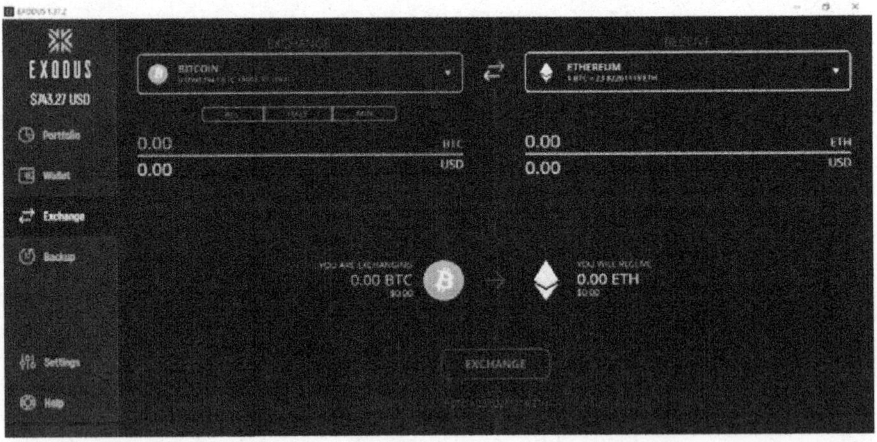

You see that there is a drop down for each of the two coins shown. You can set which coins you want to exchange between and what amounts you want.

Let's get some Ethereum into this wallet.

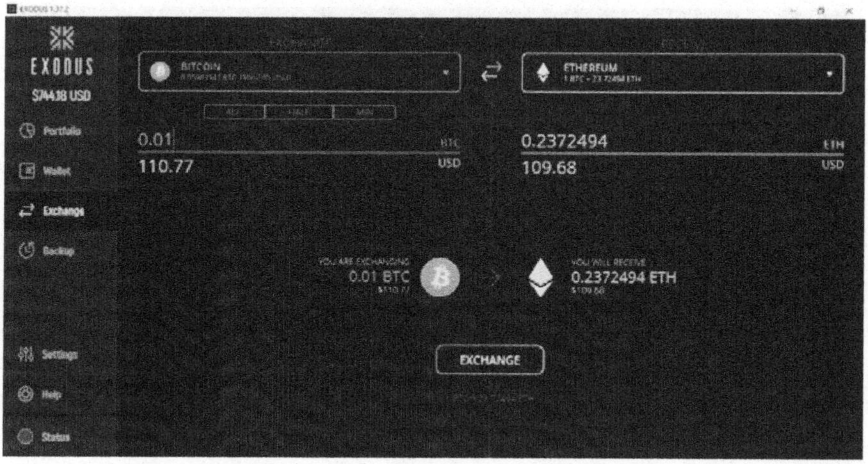

I set the amount to exchange as 0.01 Bitcoin and it automatically determines a few things. You can see that it uses the current exchange rate between BTC and ETH and calculates exactly how much Ethereum I would get for 0.01 BTC.

You'll also notice that there is a slight discrepancy between the two dollar amounts. That's the fee for this transaction.

All I need to do is to click "Exchange" and it initiates the transaction. In just a few seconds the screen moves to Step 2 and you can see a few interesting things have happened.

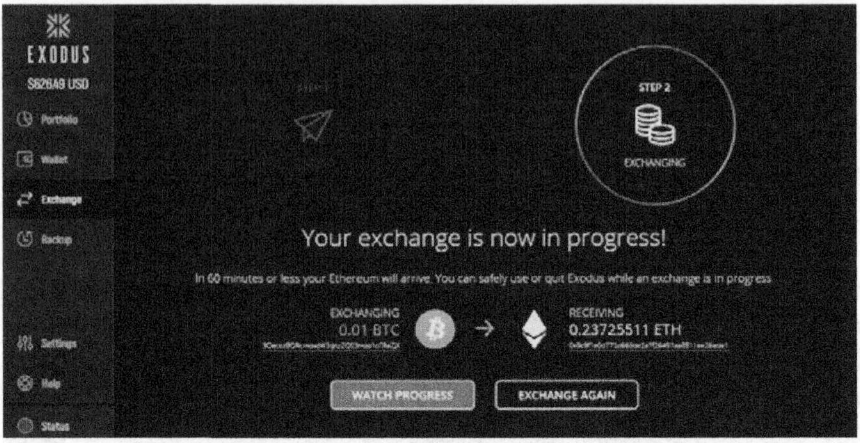

So, I've sent 0.01 BTC and I'm waiting on receiving some ETH. But actually, the amount of ETH I am now expecting has gone up a little bit. It was 0.2372494 and now it's 0.23725511.

In just those few seconds, the exchange rate changed and it recalculated the new amount. And it worked out in my favor—I'll be getting a little more than I expected!

Notice something else here. There is a "Watch Progress" button. If we click on that, it opens a window in your Internet browser and shows the engine behind this process.

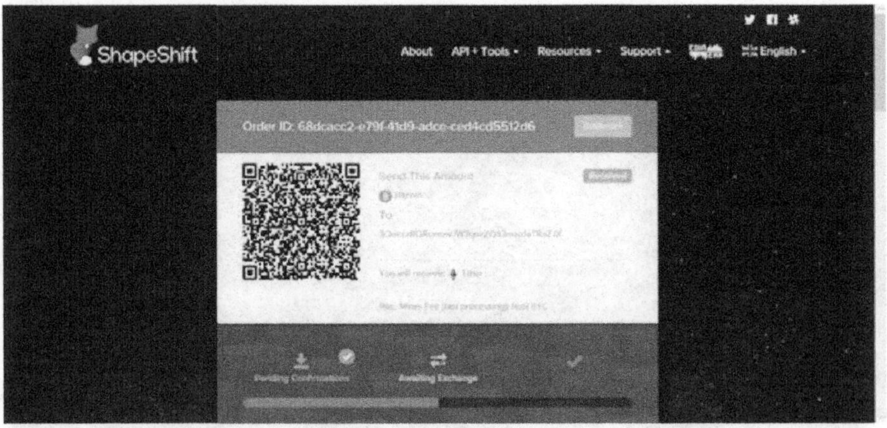

Shapeshift is the third-party service that manages the actual exchange of coins for Exodus. Here you can see the transaction ID, the address the Bitcoin was sent to, and you can monitor the status of the transaction.

But let's go back and look at something else. Go back to the "Portfolio" tab and look at the total amount of the portfolio. It's gone down by the amount of Bitcoin sent out in the transaction.

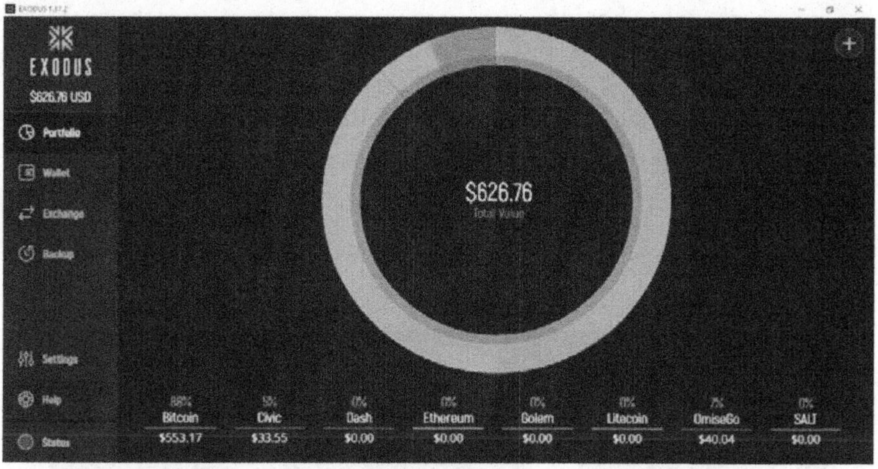

Just to be sure, open the Wallet tab and look at the Bitcoin balance.

It tells you exactly what's going on. Basically, I've sent out some

Bitcoin and I'm waiting for the equivalent value to come back in a different form.

That might feel a little scary as you just sent out some money and you don't know if or exactly when it's coming back. This is a normal procedure in crypto. It is a little different from our traditional financial experiences. It just takes some getting used to.

A little while later and I notice that the total value of the portfolio has gone back up by about the same amount it went down after the exchange was initiated.

There is a new section of white on the ring representing Ethereum and there is an amount of Ethereum shown on the bottom where before it was zero.

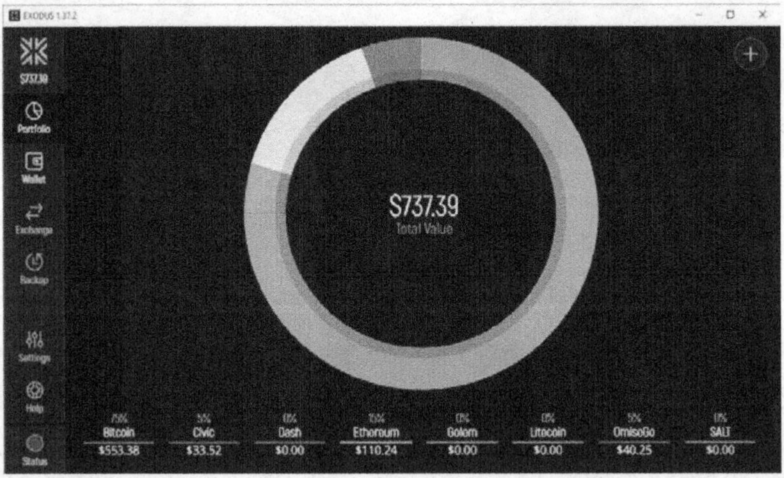

If I open the Wallet tab and click on the Ethereum wallet, I see that I now have 0.23725511ETH. Transaction complete!

This is a great feature that Exodus has, but it's only a small taste of all the possibilities out there.

Security for Your Investments

Security of your investments is something we will stress, to a certain extent, cryptos are about autonomy and personal responsibility. We want to maintain control of our financial lives, personal information, money, and wealth.

But with greater autonomy comes greater responsibility. This is where security comes in. When it comes to your cryptos, you must be responsible for them yourself. At the core of cryptocurrencies is the idea that we as a society and as individuals are ready for a "trustless" financial system. That means that we don't have to rely on (or trust) third-party providers for everything we do in our financial lives.

Banks, government agencies, insurance companies, credit card companies, and just about every website or app we use needs some kind of personal or financial information from us in order for us to use their services.

Cryptos give us an opportunity to alleviate that problem by eliminating some of those third parties, or at least for now, reducing our reliance on them.

Keeping Watch on Our Coins

I talked earlier about keeping your coins secure, but I will reiterate that here:

• Always keep your passwords, passphrases, private keys private—don't share them with anyone

• Keep your devices secure—use firewalls, anti-virus and anti-malware wherever appropriate

• Keep your devices offline or turned off whenever you're not using them

• Always backup everything—passwords, wallets, devices

Remember the distinctions I made between hot and cold, and different types of wallets? Think hard about what your goals are with your coins and how you intend to use them. When you have identified your particular needs, find the right tools that help you achieve your goals.

All that will have an impact on how secure your coins are. Now, a basic rule when it comes to cryptos is that you don't have control of your coins unless you have the private key.

Any coins you leave on an exchange is essentially controlled by the exchange. They are your trusted third party. If anything happens to the exchange, you may lose your coins.

As a rule of thumb, you don't want leave your coins on an exchange if they're not going to be actively traded. It's best to withdraw them into a secure wallet that you control.

Legality and Regulations

One of the most common questions for those new to Bitcoin and cryptocurrencies is whether or not they are legal. There are many negative stories in the media about Silk Road, ransomware, and other nefarious activities. Many people and the media often assume that Bitcoin is all part of some illegal enterprise.

Of course, that isn't true. Bitcoin is a medium that criminals use because it is more easily transferable than a suitcase full of cash and less traceable than a bank transfer. But, as you know, criminals can also use cash and bank transfers.

Bitcoin and all other cryptocurrencies and crypto assets are not illegal, except in a few outlying countries. Currently Kyrgyzstan, Bolivia, Ecuador, and Bangladesh have declared Bitcoin to be illegal. In most places in the world, however, cryptocurrencies exist in some sort of regulatory limbo where they are classed as assets, commodities, or property.

As of right now, in almost all jurisdictions, cryptos are legal to own, use, sell, or trade, but they are not technically legal as a currency.

Countries and central banks see cryptos as an innovation and don't want to squash it. But they don't want a cryptocurrency competing with their own national fiat currencies, which would weaken those currencies and reduce the government's ability to control their economies. So, we should not expect governments to make Bitcoin or any other cryptocurrency a legal currency (although it is possible).

And to keep you at ease, the trend is not toward illegalization, either, as some suggest and the media likes to hype. "China Bans Bitcoin!" is a popular joke on the various crypto forums. Outright bans of crypto coins are not likely and get less likely every day. The trend, in fact, is toward regulation. In the U.S., for example, the IRS has issued guidance on paying taxes on gains made from trading cryptos, just like any other asset. Consider this: after the FBI seized Bitcoins from illegal operations such as Silk Road, they publicly auctioned them off. The FBI would not have sold cryptos to the public if they were illegal. In fact, the FBI selling Bitcoins is a pretty good governmental indication of the legality (and future) of those assets.

Japan has just recently begun regulating and licensing crypto-exchanges. The interesting reaction from the market was that demand and trading volumes immediately began to rise—apparently, regulation is not necessarily a bad thing. China and Korea, two countries where interest in cryptos is high, have also begun to issue regulations on the cryptocurrency industry. Other countries such as the UAE, Bahrain, Singapore, The Philippines, Russia, and others are actively pursuing regulation of crypto-markets.

For now, we are free to own and transact in these crypto assets without much regulation. But regulation in one form or another is coming. However, there is no need to fear that. It's just a sign that the market is maturing. Once regulations come, we will adjust.

2018 – Year of the Altcoins

In this section, we will show how different Altcoins have their own individual (BLC) and there can only be *ONE* for each coin. Each coin's (BLC) has applications that are used in different Industry Sectors.

(CC) have made it to the headlines in newspapers as the end of 2017 is approaching. For us, this year has been a defining one.

After two full years of research and then making investments in 2017, I was able to help my closest friends with crypto investments and now I'm ready to pass the research and knowledge off to the masses.

Our most successful Altcoins over the last year were Bitcoin, Ethereum, Litecoin, Ripple, Verge, and Binance Coin. Those coins have all been bought and sold many times when the Board saw the key technical indicators in the charts. Now with our new Crypto Coin Investing Advisory program, we've been getting two main questions—which (CC) to invest in and which platform to buy from.

As you have seen in the previous chapters with my Portfolios, I'm well diversified and have a funnel of Coins of Interest and also have quite a few Altcoins in (R&D) that are in the funnel to move up when the technicals line up.

Obviously, the Altcoins in my two portfolios and Coins of interest we feel are the top coins for 2018 but we have quite a few others that are in the funnel that we feel are on the cutting edge to invest in sometime in 2018.

The following group of 15 Altcoins are in the (R&D) category and funnel that we feel we have passed Rule #1—*Problem Analysis* and Rule #2 tests—*Asset Supply Schedule.* At this point, the Board is just waiting for the technicals to line up and move them into the Coins of Interest Category or out of the funnel based on new developments. Then at some point in 2018 the Board will make the decision to invest in and move those that have moved up into the Speculative or Core Portfolio.

Our price predictions are purely speculative and these predictions most likely will be different after the book has been published and after the book release.

1. Ripple

Ripple is an open-source digital payment network which is also used by banks such as the bank of Tokyo. Call it the ripple effect, Ripple's cryptocurrency, XRP has risen a lot as well. The network is extremely fast and payments in XRP take four seconds.

Current Market Cap: **$48.2 Billion**
Markets: **Bittrex, KoinexBuy**
Order: **up to $1.3**
Our Prediction: **$5—$7**

2. IOTA

It is a (CC) designed for the Internet of Things (IoT). There is no concept of block or blockchain and thus no concept of mining. This also means that there are no transaction fees. It uses a different data structure, tangle, which is based on a directed acyclic graph.

Current Market Cap: **$11.9 Billion**
Markets: **Bittrex, Koinex**
Buy Order: **up to $5**
Our Prediction: **$20—$25**

3. Lisk

It is a public blockchain platform that provides decentralized apps. Contrary to Ethereum, it does not use solidity, and instead uses Ethereum.

Current Market Cap: **$2.8 Billion**
Markets: **Bittrex**
Buy Order: **up to $27**
Our Prediction: **$100—$200**

4. TRON

Tronix (TRX) is the official currency of TRON. TRON aims to be a decentralized entertainment content sharing platform. It will allow creators to cut down middlemen such as the Apple store and Google Play Store.

Current Market Cap: **$2.5 Billion**
Markets: **Binance**
Buy Order: **up to $0.04**
Our Prediction: **$0.15—$0.30**

5. ICON

It aims to connect organizations like Government departments, universities, hospitals and financial institutions to connect and interact without any third-party networks. This will prevent delay and avoid transaction fees.

Current Market Cap: **$1.5 Billion**
Markets: **Binance**
Buy Order: **up to $6**
Our Prediction: **$40—$50**

6. BitShares

It provides a decentralized asset exchange much like the exchanges in the real world except that these exchanges are for cryptocurrencies. It also provides a token called "BTS."

Current Market Cap: **$1.47 Billion**
Markets: **Binance**
Buy Order: **up to $0.6**
Our Prediction: **$2—$3**

7. Raiblocks

Raiblocks hopes to be an efficient alternative to fiat currencies. Like IOTA it uses a directed acyclic graph algorithm. It uses a concept called block lattice.

Current Market Cap: **$1.43 Billion**
Markets: **Mercatox**
Buy Order: **up to $12**
Our Prediction: **$40—$60**

8. Waves

Waves allow you to create multiple currency wallets and invest in verified crypto assets. This year, it has also partnered with Deloitte to launch the development of a legal framework for wider adoption of blockchain technologies.

Current Market Cap: **$1.4 Billion**
Markets: **Bittrex**
Buy Order: **up to $15**
Our Prediction: **$50—$70**

9. Stratis

Stratis is a powerful and flexible blockchain development platform. It also offers proof if an audit, proof of publication service which can be helpful for establishing ownership rights.

Current Market Cap: **$1.37 Billion**
Markets: **Bittrex**
Buy Order: **up to $15**
Our Prediction: **$50—$70**

10. Steem

Steemit is a social network that looks a lot like Medium but it pays both the content creators and the people who select the best content by up voting others' work. It's free to create an account and the content one writes will be published directly to the site.

Current Market Cap: **$800 Million**
Markets: **Bittrex**

Buy Order: **$3.5**
Our Prediction: **$15—$25**

11. Golem

Golem is an innovative idea which aims to decentralize computing power. It is a global, open-sourced supercomputer that anyone can access. Anyone can make money by renting out their computing power or developing and selling software.

Current Market Cap: **$650 Million**
Markets: **Bittrex**
Buy Order: **up to 0.8**
Our Prediction: **$2.5—$5**

12. Kyber

It is a decentralized exchange and payment service which allows instant exchange and conversion of digital assets and cryptocurrencies with high liquidity. It also provides payment APIs that allows a user to pay to a merchant in any token but the merchant will receive payment in his preferred token.

Current Market Cap: **$335 Million**
Markets: **Binance**
Buy Order: **up to $2.75**
Our Prediction: **$10—$20**

13. Powerledger

Powerledger enables peer to peer energy trading. If a person has a source of renewable energy at his home, he can trade the excess energy to somebody else and will receive payment as soon as they get energy. This allows the public to get involved in energy distribution.

Current Market Cap: **$325 Million**
Markets: **Bittrex**

Buy Order: **up to $1**
Our Prediction: **$5—$10**

14. Civic

Civic is a digital identity verification platform very much like the common "Know Your Customer" [KYC] procedure. Digital identities are stored on the blockchain and companies can do KYC very quickly. It will also pay identity verifiers i.e. banks and other trusted sources.

Current Market Cap: **$315 Million**
Markets: **Bittrex**
Buy Order: **up to $1**
Our Prediction: **$5—$10**

15. AdEx

Built on the Ethereum blockchain, AdEx is a decentralized ad exchange which aims to address problems like advertising fraud, privacy and the rise of ad blockers. It aims to be a transparent and more efficient advertising platform.

Current Market Cap: **$188 Million**
Markets: **Bittrex**
Buy Order: **up to $3.5**
Our Prediction: **$15—$30**

Here are a few more to keep an eye on in 2018:

1. **Dash**
2. **Verge**
3. **Lisk**
4. **Substratum**
5. **Cindicator**
6. **Iota**
7. **Salt**
8. **ReddCoin**
9. **Walton**
10. **Ethos**

What is "HODL" in the (CC) World?

What does HODL mean? Where did it originate? If you search the term "Hodl" in Google, you can find many memes and people claiming to be the culprit behind the term!

Some say the phrase or word originated in a chat group, some say it was from a TV show, I have even heard that the phrase originated from song lyrics!

In doing research I found out the real origin and meaning behind the word! Simply put, the phrase means "Hold" as in "hold your position."

The origin of the term comes from a (BC) forum post on Dec/18/2013 where a guy by the name of "GameKyuubi" posted about how he is a "BAD" trader and how he can't spot the "Highs" or the "Lows" like other traders could.

He also stated that weak people gave up their coins when the times were rough! He states that "Day traders can only take your money if you sell," so instead of losing money trying to day trade, or even learn how to, our friend "GameKyuubi" decided to ride the wave and "Hold" his coins.

In a way, this meant that he was a winner. A strong minded person who refused to sell because of emotion. In the crypto space one thing is clear and important. Always leave emotions out of your investments!

By the end of his rant he let everyone know that he had some whiskey and was drunk! Little did he know that he would misspell the title and unintentionally create a term so widely used in the crypto world.

The title he was going for was "I AM HOLDING" he misspelled holding and wrote "I AM HODLING."

With the misspelling of HODL— It now stands for:

"HOLD ON FOR DEAR LIFE!"

We are not quite sure where he is at this time. But, if he stuck with his plan of "HODL" since December 2013, he is probably living on his own island drinking whiskey or piña coladas with umbrellas! God bless him for his insight.

PART 3: NOW IT'S TIME TO GET IN THE GAME!

Investing: Day—Night—Short & Long Term

Well, now you know enough to be dangerous and get yourself in trouble. I can say at this point is just "Don't be stupid." Just make intelligent decisions with your investments in this "New Asset Class" of Digital Coins.

Now that we have that stuff out of the way, let's work on making our first trade.

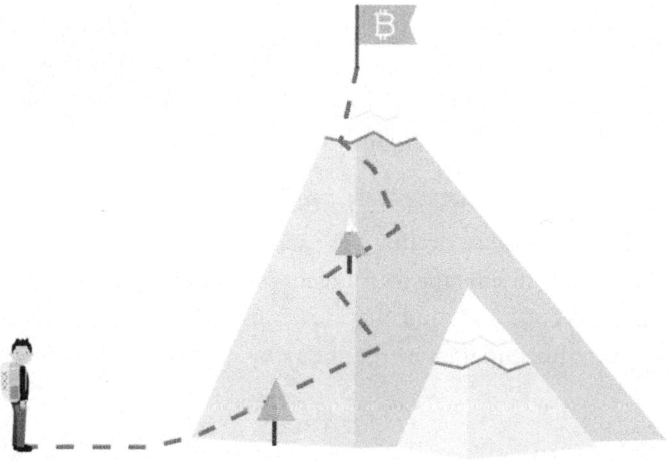

Earlier we discussed Coinbase which is the #1 exchange as of today. In this guide we will focus on two very popular exchanges, GDAX and Poloniex.

Exchanges are what allows us to buy and sell (CC). There are a handful of popular crypto-exchanges, some of them have advantages over others. For example, some exchanges don't allow us to deposit and withdraw using fiat currency like the U.S. dollar and euro; others aren't available in certain countries. In this guide, we will focus on two very popular exchanges, GDAX and Poloniex. GDAX gives us the ability to use our fiat currency to buy (BC). Poloniex does not, but does give us a wide array of altcoins to trade. There, we'll be using major coins like (BC) and Ethereum to buy the altcoins, and vice versa. Other popular exchanges such as Kraken and Bittrex offer even more coins.

Keep in mind that keeping the number of coins that you are trying to follow to a manageable amount is going to make trading a lot easier.

A "manageable amount" is obviously subjective and will vary for each person based on things such as time available to dedicate to trading. Feel free to do your own research to find the right exchange for you. I tend to value user experience of an exchange over the number of coins on it. Ultimately, what exchanges you use is going to depend on your own personal preferences. GDAX and Poloniex will provide sufficient resources needed to be a successful trader, so they are definitely a good place to start.

No matter which you choose you will need to go through a verification process when signing up for your accounts. This sometimes involves submitting a picture of your ID All in all, it's usually a pretty straightforward process and shouldn't take more than a few minutes.

The next thing we'll need to do is deposit fiat currency into our account. The easiest way to do this is by adding a bank account. Once you've initiated the deposit, it will take four business days to appear in your account. Kind of a bummer, I know; but the idea is to only need to do this once, as we'll be growing this initial investment day by day with our trades.

Order Types:

When buying or selling on crypto-exchanges, you have three different types of order at your disposal. You should be comfortable with each of them in order to be a successful trader.

Note that all orders have fees on them, though they are relatively small. Market orders allow us to exchange any amount of coin right away at the current market price. Orders are filled using the best available price in the exchange's order book. For example, if you placed a market BUY order for $100, it would buy from the lowest priced sell order(s) until you had used that $100. The advantage is that this transaction is always completed immediately; the disadvantage is that we don't know exactly what price we are going to get.

Limits orders allow us to place an order at a specific price. We can specify the amount of coin that we want to buy or sell, at the price that we want this to happen at. You may have noticed that the order book is always full of sell orders that are a little higher than the current price and buy orders that are a little lower. The advantage with limit orders is that we can do the same with our orders. The disadvantage is that our transaction likely will not be filled immediately and will count on the market price to make its way toward us.

Stop limit orders are really only useful when selling coins. They allow us to set a condition: we specify a price, and if the price becomes less than or equal to that price, a market order is automatically placed for us. The advantage here is that if we need to step away and will not be able to watch the price, we have some protection if the market begins to plummet. The disadvantage is that we are counting on the availability of good buy orders to fulfill our sell orders. If a massive amount of market sell orders were to be executed right before your stop is triggered, it's technically possible to be left with the bottom of the barrel. This has happened before, but is not common.

I can't emphasize this enough: Trading (CC) is all about minimizing losses and maximizing gains. We're not going to win every time. We'll need to utilize these various order types to do that to the fullest.

Making Our First Trade:

Once our GDAX account has been verified, and we've deposited some fiat currency we can finally make our first (BC) trade!

Here we are placing a market order. Notice that $100 would get us about 1% of a (BC). Remember that with a market order, the amount of (BC) may differ slightly from the estimate here because the price of (BC) is constantly fluctuating.

Now imagine we've seen some indication that we are ready to sell.

A small loss, but perhaps the price was about to fall, in which case we got out just in time, minimizing our loss. We've made our first trade, simple as that!

Wallets:

Wallets were discussed earlier, and we introduced a few ways and the benefits of each. We mentioned the various exchanges and now we need a way to transfer our (BC) between them. Wallets allow us to send and receive (BC).

Creating accounts on GDAX and Poloniex gives us wallets that we can send (BC) between. Let's walk through sending (BC) from GDAX to Poloniex.

First, we need the deposit address of our Poloniex wallet. Find this by going to Balances, and then Deposits & Withdrawals:

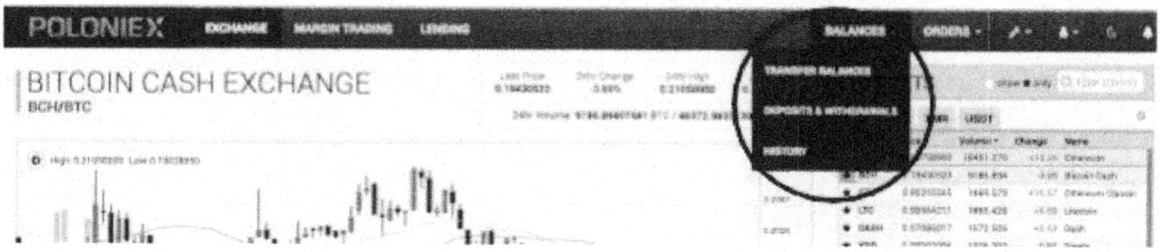

Next, we'll go to GDAX and initiate a withdrawal.

Fill in the amount of (BC) you'll be transferring, and paste the address that you copied from your Poloniex wallet in as the destination.

Be careful to put the correct address because there's no getting your (BC) back if sent to the wrong address.

Once the transfer is initiated, it could take some time for it to be verified on the [BLC]. It's not uncommon for it to take 15 minutes or more. Scaling and faster transaction speed is one of the major technical issues that (BC) and others are trying to solve.

Trading techniques that will grow your investment:

There are several proven ways to make money trading (CC). A lot of these techniques have been proven by their use on the traditional stock market. But the thing with traditional stocks is that you'd be hard-pressed to find the same kind of price swings as we see every day with (CC).

Consistent and significant price fluctuations mean more opportunities for us.

To use these techniques, we need to understand how to read charts.

Fundamentals of reading charts:

If you've already opened up GDAX or some other exchange and you were overwhelmed at first, don't worry; you weren't alone. They're called candlestick charts.

Soon, we'll learn what you can do to perform a more technical analysis on these charts, and some things that you can look for to make informed decisions during your trading. For now, let's go over some of those techniques we were talking about before.

Using stop limits to trail a bull run:

Trailing a bull run using stop orders is one of the most important techniques you can learn.

Let's do a case study. Here, I've taken a 24-hour chart for Ethereum:

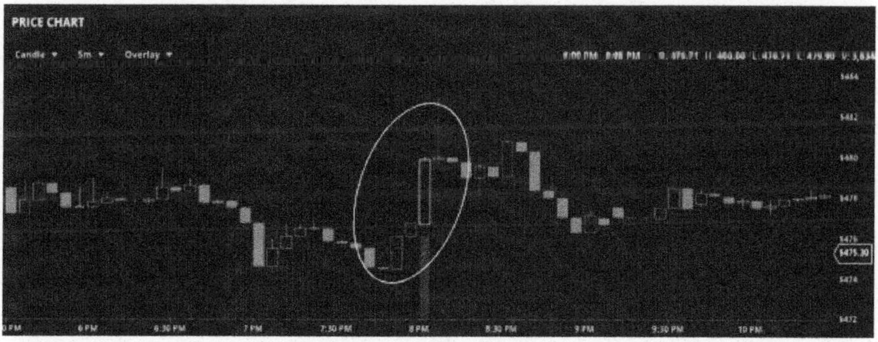

Notice the small bull run. Now imagine we had decided to buy Ethereum somewhere around that dotted line and just before 8 p.m. We saw it tick up after a string of bearish candles, and for whatever reason, thought it might continue its way upward. To minimize our losses (remember our goal is to minimize losses and maximize gains), we set a stop order right away. We'll set it near the bottom of those last couple bearish candles (about $474).

Now, as we've watched the price work its way up, we would continue to raise our stop price. To do this, we would go to our open orders (every exchange will show this) and click cancel on the stop limit that we had just set. Shortly after 8 p.m., we might've had a stop at $480 that would've been triggered. If your stop limit is triggered and the signs point to the trend continuing, you're able to buy back in with a profit already in your pocket.

We were protected, setting ourselves up for a quick profit, while at the same time being prepared for a huge profit if the price continued skyrocketing. This is the idea behind what can be a very powerful technique.

Evaluating a Coin:

When buying (CC), specifically altcoins, it is important to know a few details about them.

A major thing to note when evaluating a coin is its functional use cases. Most coins will have some form of mission statement on their homepage. By understanding what purpose a coin serves in the real world, we will have a better idea of how to evaluate it further.

For example, there are (CC), such as Litecoin, with the same goal as (BC). In this case, it would be a good idea to compare its market capitalization with (BC). This site ranks coins by market cap. Always be sure to check there when evaluating a new coin. If you notice a large shift in market cap on a certain date, it may be worth it to check for any news that day to see what may have caused it.

On the other hand, some coins serve a very unique function in the real world. For example, Power Ledger is a fairly new and interesting (CC). The goal of this project is to provide a system for consumers to trade electricity with one another. For a young project such as this, the best thing you can do is first decide whether you believe in the technology and the team behind it. The second thing you can do is read news surrounding the project. All of that information, along with a look at the coin's market cap, is going to ultimately determine whether you think the technology might reach mainstream adoption, thus making an investment worth your while.

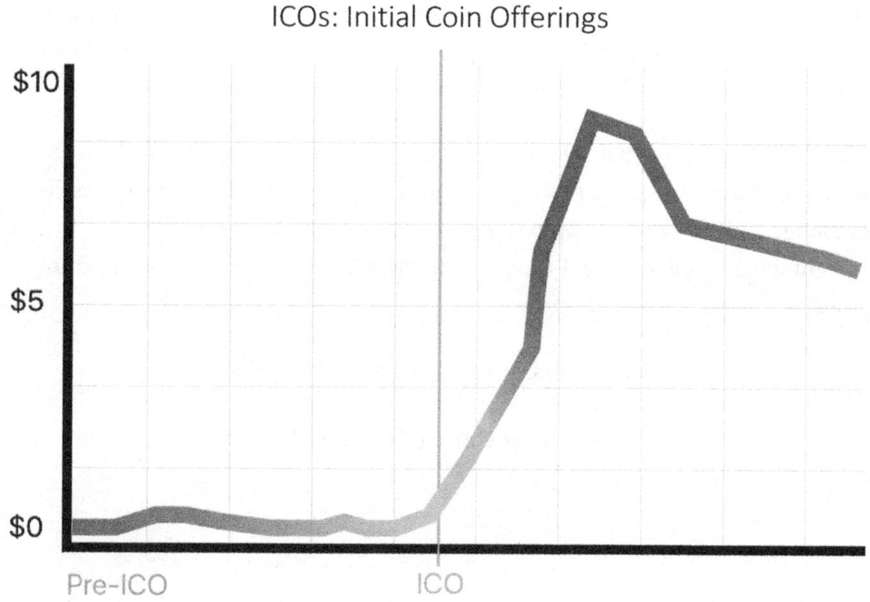

Now that we have an idea on how to get started evaluating a coin, we are better equipped to profit using another popular technique among traders.

ICOs, as you may have guessed, are much like IPOs. This is where coins are offered for the first time to the public. ICOs are not offered through exchanges, but rather you buy them directly from the creators of the project. Usually (it's different for each project) you will send them (BC) or Ethereum that they will use to fund their project; in turn you receive a certain amount of their new coin.

One of the best resources for finding out about current or upcoming ICOs is here. If you see a coin that piques your interest, be sure to be extra diligent when evaluating it. Since we have no historical data to gage how the coin might perform, it's very important to understand the real-world purpose of the coin. Another thing to note is whether the ICO is capped or not. Some ICOs will be capped at a certain number, meaning that people who are late to the party will need to wait for the coin to be offered on exchanges.

Make sure to read up on all the information that you can find, including the coin's white paper. It's common practice for coins to have one up on their site, explaining the technical details on how they plan to accomplish their goal. As you read it, see if you can determine whether you think those goals can be accomplished by the team or not.

The reason that we, as traders, would want to invest in these coins at their cheap initial price is simple: Once these coins do become available on exchanges, all of those people who missed out on the ICO will want to buy in right away. This can lead the price to skyrocket in a very short amount of time.

As traders, we will take a 10% quick

profit any day of the week.

Margin Trading & Short Positions

So far, everything we've discussed has involved taking a long position on a coin. That is, our focus has been buying a coin at a lower price than what we think we will be able to sell it at later. What if we have some indication that leads us to believe that the value of a coin is about to decrease? In this case, we could take a short position, which is the same technique that made some people boatloads of money during the 2008–2009 housing bubble.

To be able to take short positions, we need to understand margin trading. Trading on margin means we are trading with borrowed money. On exchanges like Poloniex, we can trade Bitcoin with a handful of coins (there are fewer coins offered for margin trading) with 2.5x leverage. That is, if we own 1 BTC, we can borrow up to 2.5 BTC to trade with. To be clear, this is not 2.5 BTC that we own. Now, on a trade that nets us 10% profit, we are bringing home .25 BTC instead of .1 BTC.

Like any other loan, this borrowed Bitcoin must be paid back with interest. On losses, you will need to pay back the loss and the interest. Poloniex offers up a great guide to margin trading that explains everything you need to know. It's worth reiterating that the estimated liquidation price is the price at which a forced exit from our position would occur, costing us all of the (BC) in our margin account so that it may be used to pay back the borrowed coin. Utilizing stop limits to avoid this is almost always a good idea.

It is NOT recommended to be taking long positions

on a margin trade as an inexperienced trader.

So, let's take our hypothetical 1 BTC from before and take a short position on Ethereum. We are able to borrow 2.5 BTC worth of ETH and sell it. Thirty minutes later, the price of ETH has plummeted 10%. Now we can close our short position, buying back 2.5 BTC worth of ETH; except now, since the price has dropped, we are buying more ETH than what we sold. Our borrowed coin can be paid back and we take the rest as profit!

Arbitrage:

The idea here is simple: we're going to buy a (CC) on one exchange, and sell it on another. You may have noticed that the price of a (CC) is often not the same on each exchange. How to take advantage of this is best described in this post.

Sure, it can be difficult to have a constant eye on the price of a coin on every exchange. Luckily, traders have already built bots that can help and open sourced them for others to use.

When to Buy, and Sell

We've come a long way in our path to becoming crypto-traders, but there are still some very important things to learn. So far, we've learned how to do a fundamental analysis of a (CC), and that it's important to do this so that we fully understand them before investing. But as traders, we need to understand what kinds of things tell us when we should buy or sell. We need to understand technical analysis.

What Is Technical Analysis?

Technical analysis is the study of past price patterns. This will allow us to identify opportunities for profit. The (CC) market, maybe more than any other market, has a herd mentality. The tendency, especially with inexperienced traders, is to buy when the price is rising, and sell when the price is dropping. We can take advantage of this with technical analysis.

This skill is much tougher to nail down than fundamental analysis. In today's world, everyone should be able to read up on a (CC) and stay up to date with news because all the information is at our fingertips. To become a truly successful trader, we need to be using both fundamental and technical analysis all the time.

Bottom line: technical analysis is not a strategy. It is one of the tools we will use to help execute our strategy.

Identifying an opportunity does not mean you should dump 100% of your funds into a coin.

Indicators:

Remember those candlestick charts that we see on every exchange? By studying them, we can find indicators, and understanding what these indicators mean can help us better predict the future price of the chart. There are tons of indicators and they can take some practice to become adept at identifying. You may find it easier to focus on practicing to identify them one by one until you become comfortable with them, slowly building your repertoire until you feel you're ready to go full board with your trading career.

Trends:

Technical analysis is built on the assumption that the market is trending upwards or downwards. Trends alone are usually not a great reason to buy into a trade.

If you buy when a coin is trending upwards, and sell when it looks like it's trending downwards, you're feeding into the herd mentality that I was talking about earlier. I recommend staying away from that as much as possible; it's too easy to get burned doing it.

With that being said, trends are important to spot and you can learn the process of tracing them on our membership website.

Volume:

This is a measure of the amount of a cryptocurrency that is traded over a certain period of time. Like trends, this alone is not a great reason to buy into a trade.

The best way to use volume is to determine whether a rally (the price is trying to come back up from a dip) is real or phony. For example, if a price begins to climb, but the volume does not jump with it, you can usually expect that rally to be short-lived. Our membership website explains more how to use the volume indicator.

Moving Averages:

The simple moving average (SMA) is an indicator that can help us better see price trends. It smooths out all the price fluctuations, giving a nice smooth visual. Each point is calculated by taking the average over a given period. So, the higher number you set as your period length, the smoother of a trend line you'll see.

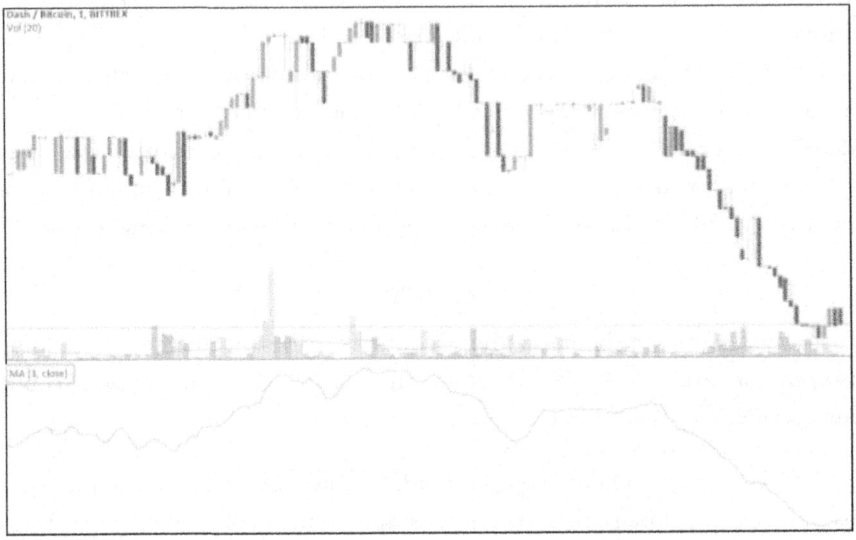

In the image above, you can see a candlestick chart for the (CC) Dash, followed by its simple moving average with a period length of 3. Notice how we are still seeing the price fluctuations? Let's increase that period length and smooth things out for a more general trend.

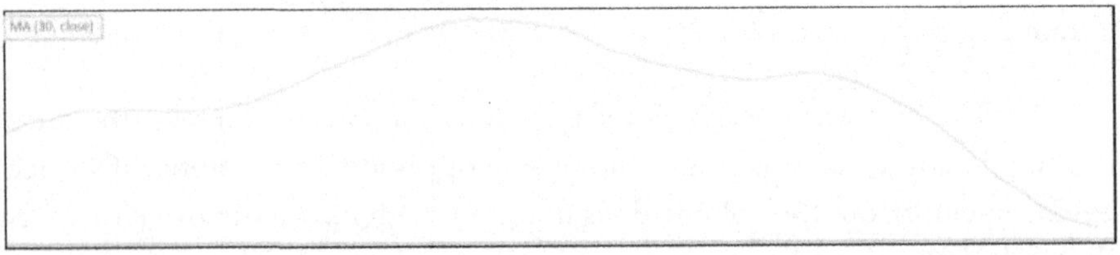

With a period length of 30, we have a much cleaner trend to go off of. The exponential moving average (EMA) on the other hand, hugs the price a lot tighter. Obviously, this alone does not tell us much that we don't already know. We need to see how to use the SMA and EMA together to tell the story of a chart.

The short version is that if we see the EMA cross above the SMA and begin shooting upwards, we know that the price is beginning to beat the trend, forcing the trend to change directions. This can make these cross points a good entry point for a trade. Similarly, a good exit point for a trade is usually when the EMA crosses below the SMA.

MACD:

Moving average convergence divergence is another useful indicator that can tell us how the momentum (the rate of change of the price) of the market is changing. The market needs volume and momentum to continue driving a price up. So, understanding which direction momentum is going, can give us an indication where the price will go.

RSI: Relative Strength Index:

RSI is another great momentum indicator to help us identify out-of-the ordinary prices, giving us an opportunity to try and take advantage of that.

Patterns:

There are tons of patterns out there and some of them can get kind of complicated. I'm going to link a few patterns that are more on the simple side that are tried and true by other crypto-traders.

Fibonacci Retracement—shows an asset's common areas of market support and resistance

Symmetrical Triangle—can help indicate the continuation of a trend or the reversal

Ascending Triangle—indicates a bullish pattern

Descending Triangle—indicates a bearish pattern

Flags and Pennants—indicates a second sharp movement following a recent sharp movement

Head & Shoulders Top—indicates reversal after an uptrend

Head & Shoulders Bottom—indicates reversal after a downtrend

If you really have an affinity for patterns and want to learn more, our member website probably lists every pattern that you can imagine.

Moving average alone can often work alone as an indicator, but it's much better to have more support from other indicators, like volume, to confirm.

Position Sizing:

Position sizing will be an important part of our next topic, which covers strategies. We need to decide how much of our capital we're going to invest for each trade (we call this taking a position). There are tons of different position sizing methods. Decide on one that works for you and stick with it.

One Position per Fixed Amount

Example: Take one Position for every $100. This means you won't be able to take two positions until you have $200.

Good for: trading with smaller sums. This is because other models may have you splitting your capital to take multiple smaller positions. Fees can hurt you on tiny positions.

Equal Position Sizes

Example: Take X equal sized positions. So, if you have $1000 and want to be able to take 5 positions, each position size will be $200.

Good for: trading with larger sums (e.g. over $5000) because it's easy to manage. You know the set amount for each position and can easily see how much you are profiting at any moment. If you have two positions with different sized, you have to do some math to find your current profit.

Downside: If you see an opportunity that is exceptionally promising, your profit may be restricted since every position must be sized equally.

Percent Risk

Example: Only risk X% of capital. So, if you have $1000 and you find two opportunities, you can take one at $750 and one at $250. Then you'll set a stop limit at 1% on each, giving you a risk of $7.50 + $2.50 = $10.00 which is 1% of $1000.

Good for: taking as many positions as you want, all at varying sizes.

Downside: difficult to manage. If you have two positions with different sizes, you have to do some math to find your current profit.

Build a Strategy and Stick to It

Let me be clear: picking out indicators arbitrarily and running with it is not going to be profitable in the long run. Crypto-traders need strategies and they need to be persistent with them.

A strategy should answer four questions:

1. How to protect your capital when the market turns against you
2. How or when to take profits
3. How much to buy or sell when you get a signal
4. When the strategy works and when it fails.

A solid strategy will give us leeway to be wrong

in half of our trades and still profit.

Read this if you don't believe me.

You've probably heard the term "risk-to-reward ratio" before. The idea in this context is that you find an opportunity where you can possibly make a 2% profit on a trade. You're going to invest $100. You set a stop limit 1% below the buy in price, so you are only risking $1, but you can make $2 on the trade. Your risk to reward ratio there is 1:2.

We use this concept to answer questions #1 and #2 when building out our strategies. Let's take a look at an example of a very common trading strategy called the breakout strategy.

A great framework for the breakout strategy uses a 1:2 risk to reward ratio. So, we would answer our four questions as follows: 1. Set a 1% stop below entry price. 2. Set a 2% buy above entry price. 3. Buy and sell full position from the start 4. Works well when the market is ranging. Does not work well when market is showing any sharp trends.

There are many other proven strategies for trading. Here are a few of them:

Reversal strategy

Pullback strategy

Moving momentum strategy

Bull flag breakout strategy

Fundamental news strategy

Follow the news. Things posted on reddit, Twitter and especially the national news can move the price. Use stop limits to protect your position.

This is worth repeating: finding a strategy that works for you and sticking to it is maybe the most important thing you can learn to do on your path to being a successful crypto-trading.

It might also be one of the toughest. You are not going to win all of your trades. Probably not even a majority of them. But as long as your account is growing, there's no reason to fix it because it's not broken.

Common Mistakes and How to Avoid Them

We did it! We made it through all the fundamentals needed to start trading (CC). I think you might agree that each individual concept on its own is not terribly complicated. You might even be thinking: "This sounds really easy! I'm going to be a millionaire by Christmas!" It's great to be ambitious about getting started, but slow your roll. It's going to take some work to put all of these concepts together, and the only way to do it is to start trading.

When you're in the thick of things, with real money on the line, you're going to make some mistakes. There's no living trader that can honestly say that they are perfect at it.

We'll close this guide with a few of the most common mistakes, and what you can do to avoid them.

Stay Level-Headed:

Perhaps the deadliest mistake a trader can make is letting emotion get the best of them. Those with the wrong mindset will lose in the long run; Whether it's losing a trade and trying to get it all back by chasing a phantom opportunity that was never really there, or winning a huge trade just to get too greedy and giving it all right back. Set a clear goal each time you sit down to trade and walk away once you've hit your goal. Do the same for losses. Walk away and come back tomorrow. There will be opportunities the next day, I promise.

One percent profit every day is a great goal. On an initial investment of $1,000, compounded at 1% profit every day for one year would grow to $37,783.43! Stay level-headed and let compounding profit work for you.

Properly Protect Your Investment:

Stop Limits. That's really all there is to say here. Too many traders fail because they don't set proper stop limits. This is an easy fix so don't let it happen to you.

Be Sure the Opportunity Is Solid:

As we learned before, identifying one identifier does not make an opportunity. Technical analysis is your friend. If you're trading with the breakout strategy, and you see a pattern that signals a possible breakout forming, use multiple indicators like volume and RSI to verify your hypothesis. If you check for three indicators and two of them confirm your hypothesis, only then should you feel confident opening a position.

On the other hand:

Don't Overanalyze It! Technical analysis is not the be-all end-all of trading. It's a tool to help you. Studying charts for hours trying to find patterns is not what's going to make you money. Zooming in from a 15-minute chart to a 5-minute chart to find a pattern that's not there is probably going to lose you money. Technical analysis works a good amount of the time, but don't blindly follow it. If signals point to a trade that you don't feel right about, it's best to trust your gut and live to fight another day.

There will be times that all signs point to a breakout that just doesn't happen. The market is made up of people and people can be irrational. Just continue to keep it simple; find a strategy or two that work for you and roll with it.

Invest What You Can Afford to Lose:

We all should know this rule, but it bears repeating. There are too many stories of people leveraging everything, even taking out second mortgages on their house, to put in cryptocurrencies. This is a very bad idea, not specifically for cryptocurrencies, but for any investment. Be smart and happy trading!

SUMMARY

Let's Review. This book is dedicated to the 3rd millennium "New Age Investors." Individuals who are set to believe in the process and will stop at nothing to get there.

So, we have now learned the history of the "NEW ASSET CLASS" and we know a lot more about how it started and how it has evolved so quickly into an industry that is rapidly gaining on the Money World Market's 86.6 Trillion Dollar industry and the World Stock Market's 66.8 Trillion Dollar industry. The (CC) Market is continually doubling its size at a rapid & record-setting pace and could easily in the very near future make it to #1.

Bitcoin is "Just the Beginning"

Jump In—Get in the Game

It's Early 1st Quarter

Next, we received the information on how to get started in this exciting and riveting new investing in a "NEW ASSET CLASS." We now have enough knowledge on how to make our investment turn into a profitable income source and if we really want to "Get Started."

As some of my closest friends have said to me many times over the years "It's time to s… or get off the pot" (R Rated). The (PG13) version would be "Take the Big Leap!"

So, what's your answer to the

"MILLION DOLLARS" question?

- All In?
- Toe in the Water?
- I need to think about it?
- Doing more (R&D) while on the sidelines?
- Monday Night Quarterback Virtually Profiting Everyday?

Whatever your decision is—works for me.

I'm glad you made it to the end since this is my first book as an author. My Philosophy in life is "If you're happy I'm happy!"

So, if "You're in the Game" or "Not in the Game" but still curious it's time we discussed some more steps in the process.

Step 1:

Go to www.cryptosecretinfo.com/bookbonus to claim your "FREE" Elite Platinum Membership Access.

Step 2:

Gain more knowledge from our membership site and other sources you find on your own individual (R&D) that we will make you smarter and more sophisticated in your investing decisions.

Step 3:

If you've made it this far and are so stoked about this.

"PLEASE TELL YOUR FRIENDS"

We are here for you if you need us!

Just shoot us an e-mail

secretsource@cryptosecretinfo.com

Made in the USA
Monee, IL
05 November 2026

68030320R10069